THE VERY SMALL
HOME

THE VERY SMALL
HOME

Japanese Ideas for Living Well in Limited Space

Azby Brown

with a foreword by Kengo Kuma

KODANSHA INTERNATIONAL
Tokyo • New York • London

NOTE: Original metric figures have been converted and rounded off, creating slight discrepancies in rare cases.

Pages 2–3: The kitchen and living room of the House in Kamakura, page 78. (Photo by Takeshi Taira)

Page 6: The sleeping loft of the House in Naka-Ikegami, page 34. (Photo by Takeshi Taira)

Foreword translated by Taeko Nanpei.
All line drawings by the author.

Distributed in the United States by Kodansha America, Inc., and in the United Kingdom and continental Europe by Kodansha Europe Ltd.

Published by Kodansha International Ltd., 17–14 Otowa 1-chome, Bunkyo-ku, Tokyo 112–8652, and Kodansha America, Inc.

ISBN-13: 978–4–7700–2999–7
ISBN-10: 4–7700–2999–3

First edition, 2005
11 10 09 08 07 06   10 9 8 7 6 5 4 3

Library of Congress Catalogue-in-Process Data available

www.kodansha-intl.com

CONTENTS

FOREWORD

Kengo Kuma

There is a short essay written in the thirteenth century that is still treasured by the Japanese today. *An Account of My Hut* was penned by the poet and literary recluse Kamo no Chomei after he took to living a refined yet simple life in a small country cottage. The image of his pastoral existence of quiet contemplation exists as an ideal in the Japanese mind to this day, and is echoed in the rise of the new small home so ably introduced by Azby Brown in the present volume.

On rereading Chomei's account of his serene lifestyle, I was surprised at the number of similarities between his age and ours. Chomei lived through a period of repeated political disturbances. The once-static world of the all-powerful aristocrats collapsed. The samurai came to power, but their rule was far from stable. The national economy was in a state of confusion, and famine was rife. Successive natural disasters—a devastating typhoon, a great fire, and a ruinous earthquake—rocked the nation, further destabilizing the lives of the inhabitants.

The last ten to fifteen years in Japan have been no less turbulent. They have seen the collapse of the conservative party that governed for fifty years from the end of World War Two. Economic confusion, the Great Hanshin Earthquake, and terrorist activities conducted by the Aum Shinrikyo religious cult have increased the general anxiety within society. Nearly eight hundred years earlier, living in similarly troubled times, Chomei erected his "ten-foot-square hut," as it is known in English, and wrote an essay on his modest dwelling that has become one of the landmarks of Japanese literature.

Perhaps, then, it is no coincidence that Japan has experienced a boom in small housing, a type of home different in every aspect from the marble-covered mansions of the "bubble economy" of the 1980s. An unassuming elegance has replaced grand showmanship. The lot size and the floor space are surprisingly small; materials are modest yet pleasing and economical.

The small abode has become all the rage in Japan. Enthusiasm has filtered into architectural journals, popular magazines, television programs, and documentaries. Every fresh development and trend is eagerly charted and explained. Critics, too, have surfaced, theorizing that the trend signals a flight from reality to the closed, private space. This, however, could not be further from the truth. Homeowners, with the assistance of talented architects, are realizing their dream of owning a home, even on a limited budget. Focusing on the essentials and a strong sense of poetry—what Azby Brown calls the Big Idea—they are creating, within finite quarters, a refined living space, generating new and important ideas.

In fact, the success of these sometimes startling designs compares favorably with the surprisingly poor efforts of the large-scale apartment complexes built over the same period. The beauty and creativity found in small home design clearly attest to its originality; stunning works have been produced, many notable for their innovations in lighting, storage, space allotment, and materials selection, as well as their effective blending of dream and reality. Indeed, within the realm of this budding residential genre, more and more architects and homeowners are finding their stride, while the designs of large-scale, urban redevelopment projects remain uninspired, second-rate reproductions of overseas originals.

For me personally, as an architect, designing small homes suggests new directions in the relationship between people and the environment, and, on a wider scale, the future of the home. In many Western countries, nature and the manmade object are treated as opposing forces; nature is viewed as a harsh, overpowering entity to be fought. The Japanese people, on the other hand, have traditionally considered nature to be weak and ephemeral, not unlike the transitory existence of life on earth; thus, we have sought to coexist with nature. The small house is, in a real sense, an experimental laboratory that permits us to pursue the creation of a complementary relationship with our surroundings.

Here, too, Chomei's work becomes a touchstone. The threads of his account run deep; his essay is much more than a simple story of a man putting up a small, humble house in an insecure world. Amid the details of his home-building (using natural materials such as bamboo, strategically placing a hedge to take advantage of the setting sun, and so on) is a growing sense of how a rich life can be fashioned from simple means as we seek to realize our vision. A fertile life was possible in "that small house," Chomei believed, *because* it was small, not "in spite of the fact that it was small." Eight hundred years later, his idea still resonates—in Tokyo, in Japan, in the pages you hold in your hand.

INTRODUCTION

Why Small, How Small?

There are many reasons for building small. Often we tend to regard a small house as a lesser creation, an indication of some want or unfortunate set of circumstances, but in fact this is not necessarily the case. A well-designed small house that has been carefully thought out and built as a matter of conscious choice in the face of alternatives is neither poor nor substandard. The need for small houses is widely recognized in Japan as well as abroad, and recent years have witnessed a surge of interest in what might be called the small-house lifestyle, and a concomitant explosion of books, articles, documentaries, and other explorations of the theme and its possibilities. And it has become widely recognized that Japan remains a leader in the field.

In Japan, it seems, everyone is in on the act. Most architects, regardless of status, are happy to try their hand at building small homes; similarly, construction companies of all sizes are asked to apply their considerable technical and organizational resources to the problem daily. The numerous Japanese prefabricated-house manufacturers have long recognized that homes of 1,100 square feet (100 sq. m.) or less are not merely for the budget-conscious entry market but represent a mature and established segment that draws in clients from all walks of life. The Japanese media seem obsessed with small houses; television specials are broadcast weekly, new book titles appear one after the other, and most significantly, an entire sector of the popular press that specializes in small-house trends and ideas has emerged. The current boom in well-designed, compact houses in Japan has been given tremendous momentum by the thorough and intelligent coverage that appears in the lifestyle and fashion magazines, so much so that for an entire generation it almost seems that a house has to be small in order to reflect good design sense. This new respectability is a bonanza for those of us who want to learn how to build small and beautifully.

All of the houses featured in this book are recent, the oldest being less than five years old at the time of this writing. As such, they represent aspects of building practice that have emerged since the end of the Japanese real estate bubble. After a period of chaos and lack of direction, the building trades seem to have found their feet and, led by the market and social trends, have had several strong years of innovation and creativity. The clients have adjusted, the designers have adjusted, and most importantly, the tradesmen and suppliers—carpenters, engineers, steel companies, window manufacturers, and others—have adjusted to make high-quality work on small houses cost effective. Most of the designers whose creativity is highlighted in these pages work on a variety of scales, including standard-sized homes, office buildings, apartment blocks, and commercial developments, but are all happy to take on small house work because these kinds of projects can be extremely gratifying creatively, and also carry a high potential for recognition, prizes, and publicity.

Clients, too, are more astute, and more rather than less demanding in terms of what they expect from small homes. It has often been remarked that Japanese value good design and are very fashion conscious, but until recently attention to home design has been lacking. Ultimately, it is the increased level of awareness on the part of the market—the clients—that drives the trend.

It is hard to imagine a much simpler house than this. A lifestyle experiment which reproduces a postwar Japanese design, the 320-square-foot (30-sq.-m.) Sumire-Aoi House is adequate for a small family.

SUMIRE-AOI HOUSE

DESIGN: Makoto Koizumi (prototype by Makoto Masuzawa)

CONSTRUCTION: wood / 2 floors

OCCUPANTS: family of four

LOT: 1,012 sq. ft. (94 sq. m.)

HOUSE: 320 sq. ft. (29.7 sq. m.)

TOTAL FLOOR AREA: 533 sq. ft. (49.5 sq. m.)

At once modern and traditional, the Sumire-Aoi House uses wood for nearly all its interior surfaces. The house works as well as it does largely because of the generous, well-lit atrium over the living space.

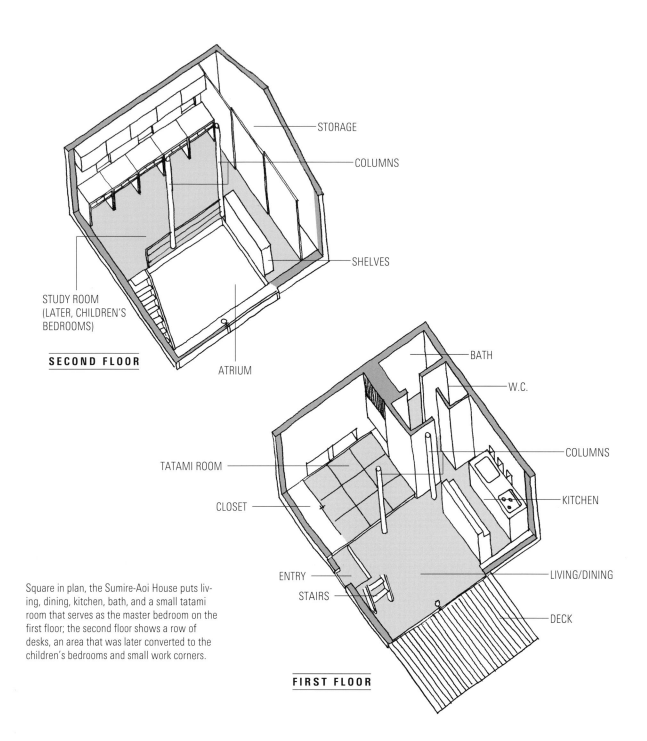

STORAGE

COLUMNS

SHELVES

STUDY ROOM
(LATER, CHILDREN'S
BEDROOMS)

SECOND FLOOR

ATRIUM

BATH

W.C.

COLUMNS

TATAMI ROOM

KITCHEN

CLOSET

ENTRY

LIVING/DINING

STAIRS

DECK

Square in plan, the Sumire-Aoi House puts living, dining, kitchen, bath, and a small tatami room that serves as the master bedroom on the first floor; the second floor shows a row of desks, an area that was later converted to the children's bedrooms and small work corners.

FIRST FLOOR

That said, there are many ways of building small, and many reasons for doing so. In the course of researching this book, I came across several homeowners for whom limiting the size of their houses represented an aesthetic choice. That is, they could easily afford larger homes but felt a smaller one would allow them to live more beautifully. Looking at the 4 x 4 House by Tadao Ando, unquestionably one of the leading architects in Japan, and the Sumire-Aoi House by Makoto Koizumi, might shed some light on the issue of choice. The Sumire-Aoi House is essentially a replica of a 1952 house by architect Makoto Masuzawa. At 320 square feet (30 sq. m.)—9 *tsubo* in traditional Japanese measure—the original was an inexpensive, minimal prototype for war-ravaged Japan, where the housing shortage remained severe. Inspirational and influential, it was a no-frills home for people who had been living in a devastated landscape in tarpaper shacks and yet hoped for something secure and affordable. Koizumi's reconstruction is something of a lifestyle experiment,

SEE PHOTOS ON
PAGES 14 AND 19

and it refers to a different kind of devastation, a real-estate landscape where home ownership is out of reach for most families. Essentially a large, single, glass-fronted room with a loft, the house has a kitchen and bath on the ground floor, room for a small dining table, and a tatami-matted room that serves as a living room in the daytime and a bedroom at night (an idea rooted in Japanese tradition). The second floor was originally constructed as an undivided balcony space, but the owners' twin daughters—the Sumire and Aoi of the house's name—requested private rooms, and a simple partition and sliding door closure was added later, also providing a tiny 22-square-foot (2-sq.-m.) office/workspace. It is a very outward looking, sunny house that is affected dramatically by its surroundings, and has many design features found in traditional Japanese homes. And it cost only about $100,000, an unbelievably low price in Japan. Since its construction, the Sumire-Aoi House has garnered a tremendous amount of publicity, and people have begun to consider living in "9 *tsubo*" viable once more. This house has lowered the bar for home ownership, and brought a previously unattainable dream somewhat closer for many. Yet accepting these limits still leaves most Japanese with mixed emotions.

With a footprint of 240 square feet (23 sq. m.), Ando's 4 x 4 House takes up about the same amount of land as the Sumire-Aoi House, though its four stories give a total floor area of 1,270 square feet (118 sq. m.). It is similarly austere and light filled, but the resemblance ends there. The client has obtained a spectacular beachfront site on the Seto Inland Sea in Kobe, and the entire design is motivated by the desire to live with a sweeping, panoramic view of the sea, Awaji Island, and the magnificent Akashi Bridge. The house stands as a slender tower, a spectacular but compact home for one. Without a whiff of poverty or want, simply the concrete realization of the desire for spiritual elevation, it is a prime example of what I call the "Big Idea" approach to small design.

In fact, most of the successful small house designs I have come across rely on one primary Big Idea: a key design feature or idea that defines the house, and to which most other aspects of the house are subordinated. In the 4 x 4 House, it is the large wall of glass on the fourth floor which brings in the panorama; in the Ambi-Flux House, it is the central atrium; in the Sora no Katachi House, the garden; in the Engawa House, the long wall that opens by means of sliding doors; in the Naka-Ikegami House, the skylight that runs the length of the house. It may be the notion of living in the treetops, as seen in both the Penguin House and the T. R. House. In others it may be a staircase, or a special room, or a view, or a wall, or the use of levels. But in every case, the designers have said, "If we let this feature live, and nourish it, then its benefits will pervade the rest of the house." And in most cases this approach yields stunning results. This is not to imply that if one element works well the rest can be ignored, for everything must mesh. But home design is largely about character, specifically about enhancing our relationships to each other, giving ourselves an environment that has a strong identity to play off of. The character may be lighthearted, or subdued, or natural, or bright, or handmade, but it is the Big Idea that does the most to suggest it. Many other features may need to be pared away in order to allow this essential character to emerge.

4 X 4 HOUSE

DESIGN: Tadao Ando
CONSTRUCTION: reinforced concrete / 4 floors + basement
LOT: 704 sq. ft. (65.42 sq. m.)
HOUSE: 243 sq. ft. (22.56 sq. m.)
TOTAL FLOOR AREA: 1,268 sq. ft. (117.79 sq. m.)

A good designer must have a deep understanding of human comfort and communication, and be on the same wavelength about these issues with his clients. As we will see, comfort is not always about space, but it is about not bumping into things; communication is not always about a wraparound sofa, but it is about having places to be together as well as alone. As I pointed out in *Small Spaces*, often comfort requires nothing more than a nice chair with a little table and an engrossing book. And if one hopes to design in a way that enhances communication, it's probably acceptable to have family members rub elbows as long as everyone can enter and leave the circle freely. In the best small-home designs, the designer has taken the time to understand the clients' daily pattern of life, to help identify the areas that work and those that don't and to share ideas with the owners to suggest a more attractive, refreshing or liberating daily life story. The design may encourage father to go up to the roof to do some gardening, or hint that an energetic child will spend most of her playtime on a sheltered deck that opens onto a common garden. It may imply that a particular table will be the center of family life throughout the day or that the act of meal preparation will be a performance. These stories may be suggested by the Big Idea, or they may be subplots that unwind around the periphery of life. But the best-conceived small house can suggest a larger, richer life and allow us to be fuller human beings. Its all about developing a design that takes our own life story and enhances the good parts, maybe adding a few passages about who we want to be.

A house must allow us to change. No matter how enticing the story, or how carefully worked out the details, if a house cannot accommodate natural human change and evolving priorities it will ultimately be less than satisfactory. Not every aspect of the house must be flexible, however; one intended for a single mature occupant will probably require less flexibility than one with growing children. Flexible storage is always a good idea. Children's sleeping areas will need to be designed with change in mind. A bath that is well designed from the outset will probably be useful for the life of the house. Kitchens tend to accumulate new appliances and crockery, but the placement and size of counters rarely change. While a new dining table is an entirely reasonable expectation, its general size and location will most probably remain set. At one extreme, entire walls may be made temporary and movable, as in the Engawa House, or a space can be built essentially open to be subdivided later, as in the Ambi-Flux House. Social space can be put to dual use as a spare bedroom, as in the Saginomiya House, or a spare room can be used as a work space initially, with the understanding that it will eventually become a child's bedroom, as in the Natural Wedge House.

Flexibility and comfort are also frames of mind. I recall visiting a Tokyo homemaker in a well-designed house that was built when her two children were small. They had grown into teens, and the family still shared a single bath with a single washbasin and mirror. As we sat at her kitchen table I asked, "Don't you and your daughter get in each other's way with your morning makeup routines?" "No, it's not a problem," she replied," because I prefer to do my makeup here. In fact I do everything sitting right in this chair." She then proceeded to demonstrate how from her preferred perch she could make tea, answer the phone, read, write, and yes, do her makeup (by propping a mirror on top of her cosmetics case, which she kept close at hand), all without getting up from her favorite chair. It was a way of doing things she had discovered and which suited her perfectly, a casual and comfortable multitasking that I doubt would have been suggested by even the most perceptive designer, and that, even if it had, would have met with indignant resistance. But this homeowner would never have gotten the idea had her kitchen not been a sunny, cozy spot from which she could keep an eye on the rest of the house to begin with.

There are a number of other essential points to consider. The importance of light cannot be overstressed. By this I don't mean having bright light everywhere. Natural sunlight is essential, since it activates and energizes the house, but there needs to be a kind of gradation of illumination, a few dark corners that lend the well-lit areas their impact. Light fixtures themselves are fun and usually deserve to be experimented with (T. R. House), while at other times hidden lighting can give a room an unobtrusive uplift (Nakagawa House). Similarly, if the circulation within a house isn't smooth, unobstructed, and nearly effortless, the house will immediately feel cramped. Little changes of direction, as in the Sora no Katachi, Kyodo, and Naka-Ikegami houses, make a home seem larger and lend it a bit of mystery, which in itself is highly desirable — the feeling that there is more to be seen. Changes in level — both floor and ceiling — are extremely useful in giving particular corners a distinct identity, and making movement through the house more interesting. Sightly raised floors may also allow additional storage to be located underneath.

Views are important, but they need not be panoramas to have a positive impact. It may be only a patch of sky, or a glimpse of garden, or even an attractive roofscape, but every house needs to feel like it opens onto the world outside. The same opening that frames the view — and it should be nicely framed, and visible from deep within the house — will let in light as well, so from the outset it is a dual-use feature. With movement through space, some modulation of light, a carefully framed view or two, a clear sense of where people can be together and where they may be alone, a natural hierarchy of space will develop. The desire for privacy may be indicated simply, perhaps with a step and a curtain; time to eat and time to work may be suggested by the orientation of seating. The most private areas — a bathroom or bedroom — could be physically closer to the entryway than living spaces that invite guests, but reached by a longer path.

Color, materials, and texture are tremendous tools. Some homes will be small enough for only a single basic palette to be used, but in most cases there is room to play. While natural materials have a lot to recommend themselves in terms of warmth and tactile attractiveness many designers prefer the extremely light colors and smooth surfaces afforded by modern synthetics. Natural and synthetic materials may be combined very well. Ideally, walls and floors will be interesting when one's eyes come to rest on them but will not clamor for visual attention; instead they will act as a foil for the things one really wants to be seen: artwork, decoration, a nice piece of furniture, the play of light on another surface, a view. Because of this, many designers have developed a style and choice of materials in which nearly everything is plain and inexpensive but attractive, and in which one or two luxurious details can set the mood of the room, often of the entire house: a fine photograph, an antique bench, exotic wood trim, some fine glass. This is an approach that has deep roots in Japanese culture, particularly in the world of the tea ceremony, where guests would be invited into a small, rustic, dimly-lit clay and thatch hut only to find an exquisite and priceless vase placed in a simple niche. The guests will remember the vase.

The houses featured in this book are, I believe, representative of the best and most interesting small-house design in Japan today. I have attempted to convey their essential character, to describe how they are organized as well as how they feel, and to discuss the intentions of the designers as well as the desires of the owners. Some are fairly conventional and others are extreme. But all are well thought out, and none were included that didn't strike me as very livable when I visited them *in situ*, even though I may have been prepared not to like them based on the photographs I had seen. The reader may not find a house in this book that will immediately seem ideal for his or her own situation, but that is not my intention. Rather, I hope to give an idea of the endless possibilities that can present themselves when one approaches building in limited space with an open mind and a fired imagination. Let the ideas presented here spark others. Dare to be small!

NOTE ON THE SELECTION: Selecting the houses to be included in the book involved a tremendous amount of research, initially by searching printed sources and approaching architects. I looked for houses in the greater Tokyo area that were recent, livable, and inspired in terms of how they coped with size constraints. After sifting through the photographs and plans of hundreds of houses, about fifty were chosen for more detailed investigation, and about thirty were actually visited. Eighteen made the final cut, which represents a mix of styles, family makeup, prominent features, and design approaches. The houses presented here range in total floor area from 540 to 1,730 square feet (50 to 160 sq. m.), although most of them fall within a range of 850 to 1,200 square feet (80 to 110 sq. m.).

The striking towerlike form of the 4 x 4 House shows just how expressive a small house can be. At first glimpse one immediately wants to climb to the top floor to experience the view.

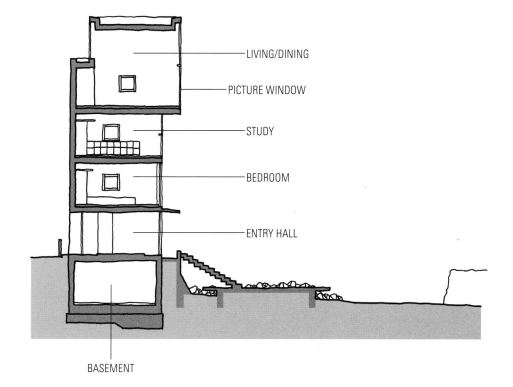

LIVING/DINING

PICTURE WINDOW

STUDY

BEDROOM

ENTRY HALL

BASEMENT

With one small floor devoted to each living function, the square-plan 4 x 4 House sacrifices easy circulation in order to gain a dramatic living space on the offset top floor.

THE HOUSES AT A GLANCE

Designing any house is an exercise in compromise; it is impossible to have every desired feature, all conveniences, every stylistic flourish. The importance of compromise only increases when space is limited; if one tries to keep the cost down as well, the challenge is greater still. But even when faced with compromise, not only is it possible to decide what to emphasize and to do it beautifully, it is essential to do so.

The following chart highlights some of the outstanding characteristics of the eighteen houses described in the following pages. None of them have marks in every category; a house that has a hobby space might sacrifice storage, and one that has good parking might do without a garden. The lack of a mark does not imply inadequacy in that particular area; rather, a mark is included when a feature is considered really well done. The "privacy" column refers less to privacy vis-a-vis the neighbors (difficult, though not impossible, to achieve in urban Japan) than to privacy for the occupants from each other. Finally, note that every house has a mark in the "good lighting" column; light is so essential to a successful small house that only beautifully-lit houses made it into the book. Similarly, though a column was not included, each small home selected for inclusion needed to be personal, poetic, and inspirational on some level.

FEATURES / HOUSES	NO. OF OCCUPANTS	NO. OF FLOORS	GOOD LIGHTING	GOOD KITCHEN	GOOD BATH	GOOD STORAGE	GOOD FOR KIDS	WORK/HOBBY SPACE	EASY FOR ENTERTAINING	PRIVACY	LOTS OF GREENERY	SHELTERED PARKING	EASILY EXPANDABLE
SAGINOMIYA	1	2	●	●		●		●	●	●	●		
NAKAGAWA	4	1	●	●	●	●				●	●		
MOTO-AZABU	2	3	●						●	●		●	
NAKA-IKEGAMI	3	2+lft	●	●		●			●			●	
UMEGAOKA	3	2+b	●	●		●	●	●					
PENGUIN	2	3	●		●			●			●		
GLASS SHUTTER	3	3	●	●				●	●				
T-SET	2	2+m	●					●		●			
SORA NO KATACHI	3	2+b	●				●	●		●	●	●	
WHITE BOX	3	2	●	●		●		●					
AMBI-FLUX	4	3 (+2)	●		●		●				●		●
NATURAL WEDGE	2	3+b	●		●			●	●			●	
T. R.	2	3	●								●	●	
KYODO	3	2	●		●	●		●		●	●		
KAMAKURA	2	2+lft	●	●				●	●		●		●
KAGURAZAKA	4	3	●			●	●				●		
ENGAWA	4	1	●	●	●	●	●				●	●	
KUGENUMA	2	2	●		●			●			●	●	

m=mezzanine, b=basement, lft=loft

PART I THE HOUSES

SAGINOMIYA HOUSE

An easy-to-maintain home to entertain in

DESIGN: Chiharu Sugi & Manami Takahashi, Plannet Works

CONSTRUCTION: reinforced concrete & wood / 2 floors

OCCUPANTS: single adult

LOT: 921 sq. ft. (85.59 sq. m.)

HOUSE: 460 sq. ft. (42.73 sq. m.)

TOTAL FLOOR AREA: 866 sq. ft. (80.41 sq. m.)

From the exterior, this house is a simple rectangular volume that fills the entire lot, with recesses to accommodate the ground floor entryway and a garden on the side. A bay window protrudes slightly from the corner above the entry.

The actual living area on the second floor feels like a single open space, the living/dining combination and the bedroom separated by the glassed-in garden. The roof of the entire living space is raised slightly so that light can spill in along the edge, giving upper floor a weightless feeling.

The compact stairway leading from the guest/party space on the ground floor to the living space above is filled with personal photos, and has a small display case for glassware on one side (*top left*) that actually opens to the small kitchen.

The entire ground floor is intended for parties and the occasional overnight guest. A full kitchen with bar seating is included, and ample natural light filters through the garden terrace.

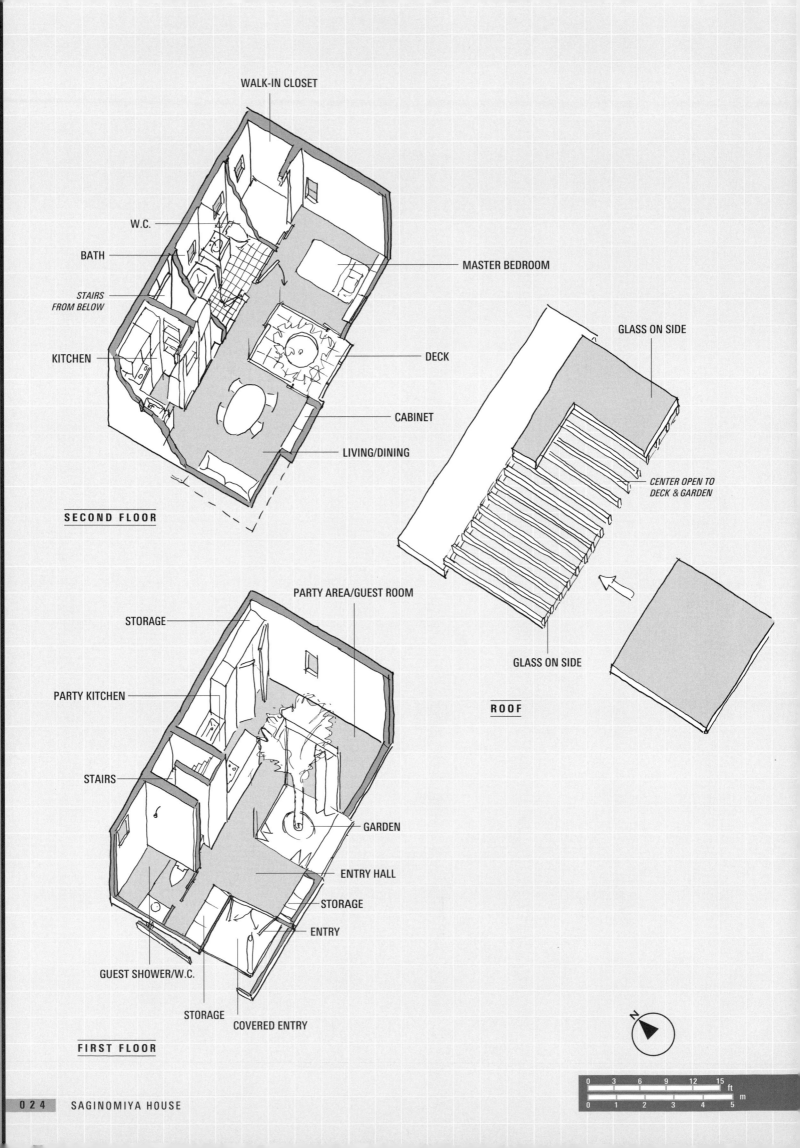

WALK-IN CLOSET

W.C.

BATH

STAIRS FROM BELOW

KITCHEN

MASTER BEDROOM

DECK

CABINET

LIVING/DINING

SECOND FLOOR

GLASS ON SIDE

CENTER OPEN TO DECK & GARDEN

GLASS ON SIDE

ROOF

STORAGE

PARTY AREA/GUEST ROOM

PARTY KITCHEN

STAIRS

GARDEN

ENTRY HALL

STORAGE

ENTRY

GUEST SHOWER/W.C.

STORAGE

COVERED ENTRY

FIRST FLOOR

N

0 3 6 9 12 15 ft
0 1 2 3 4 5 m

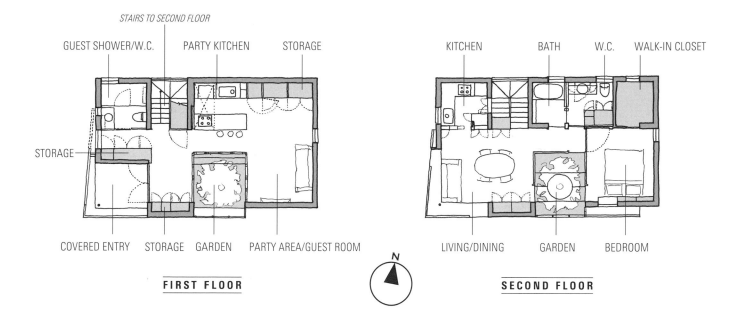

STAIRS TO SECOND FLOOR

GUEST SHOWER/W.C.   PARTY KITCHEN   STORAGE   KITCHEN   BATH   W.C.   WALK-IN CLOSET

STORAGE

COVERED ENTRY   STORAGE   GARDEN   PARTY AREA/GUEST ROOM   LIVING/DINING   GARDEN   BEDROOM

FIRST FLOOR   **SECOND FLOOR**

This house for a single retired woman is a very personal space for one. The client was clear about how she wanted to live, and selected the designers, Plannet Works, after commissioning initial proposals from several firms. She entertains frequently and has a full social life, but values her privacy and quiet. She wanted a house that would be easy for her to maintain by herself but which could accommodate overnight guests. The result is closer to a house with a separate apartment for entertaining.

The entire first floor is a party space, with a complete kitchen, a bar counter, and ample storage. There is a comfortable sofa and chairs and a large TV; the floor is easy-to-clean tile. The entire space wraps around a small garden, which acts as a light well. It is a nicely detailed and elegant evening space, with some luxurious details, but very understated. It could easily be used as an apartment for a grown child or relative, and is occasionally pressed into service as a spacious guest room.

The second floor is reached via a stairway whose walls are lined with framed pictures, all of which have personal significance for the owner. Literally climbing towards the light, one enters the owner's warm living quarters. Designed around the small garden, the living space gets light from every direction. The flat roof is raised enough to form a wraparound transom, letting illumination in and making the ceiling and its exposed beams feel nearly weightless (see detail on page 104). Wood is used extensively on this level: in cabinetry and in the wide knotty pine floorboards. The overall space is divided in two by the garden: a living/dining area, which has a big corner window with a shelf for pictures and mementos—an ideal corner for sitting— and smaller sleeping quarters. The effect is of a single light-filled space, though the bedroom has a hidden door that can be pulled from a recess in the wall when privacy is desired. The architects placed the kitchen, stairs, bath, and large walk-in closet in a row along the far side of the house, out of sight but close at hand, an excellent planning idea that gives the sense of an unobstructed living space; the straight corridor, which joins the living and sleeping areas, also provides easy access to these less frequently used areas. This configuration is so straightforward it may seem obvious, but here the materials, the height of the openings, and the alignment of this "service wall" with the transom above are handled with great awareness and give the space a comfortable coherence.

The exterior of the house is similarly handsome, finished in warm colored stucco and faded wood, and is entirely unprepossessing. Though the owner could have built a much larger, more luxuriously appointed home if she had desired, her choices reveal an admirable attitude toward life, one which the architects have skillfully allowed to be expressed in this modest, inviting house.

NAKAGAWA HOUSE
Lovingly detailed renovation for a family of four

DESIGN: Tsuneo Shimojima, Pittori Piccoli
CONSTRUCTION: steel frame & autoclaved lightweight concrete / 1 floor
OCCUPANTS: family of four
LOT: 2,153 sq. ft. (200 sq. m.)
HOUSE: 1,136 sq. ft. (105.5 sq. m.)
TOTAL FLOOR AREA: 1,123 sq. ft. (104.3 sq. m.), excluding deck

The kitchen work island is a sculptural object that acts as a room divider; high enough for privacy, it is nevertheless low enough to see over, separating without obstructing. Integrated lights and planters make it the visual centerpiece of the house. (See also detail on page 96.)

The living space is free flowing and well lit, curving around in an L shape. The white tile floor is durable and contributes to the expansive feeling.

All of the kitchen storage is fitted into a single curving wall of pull-out cabinets arranged on either side of the refrigerator. Their heights and widths vary slightly to accommodate different storage needs.

Japanese homes require a shoe cabinet of some sort near the entryway. Here, beautiful cabinetry transforms this mundane requirement into a study in minimal form. An illuminated gap provides unexpected display space for small items. (See also detail on page 100.)

One of the architect's stylistic signatures is providing witty and unexpected storage, in this case a set of small drawers fitted into a cabinet door.

The bath area takes advantage of the large deck outside to gain a sense of openness and natural illumination. One corner of the deck has been simply enclosed for privacy.

The dining area accommodates the small family and perhaps a guest or two. The designer turned a pair of existing structural columns that could not be moved into a spatial divider that helps define the dining area, integrating them with recessed ceiling lighting.

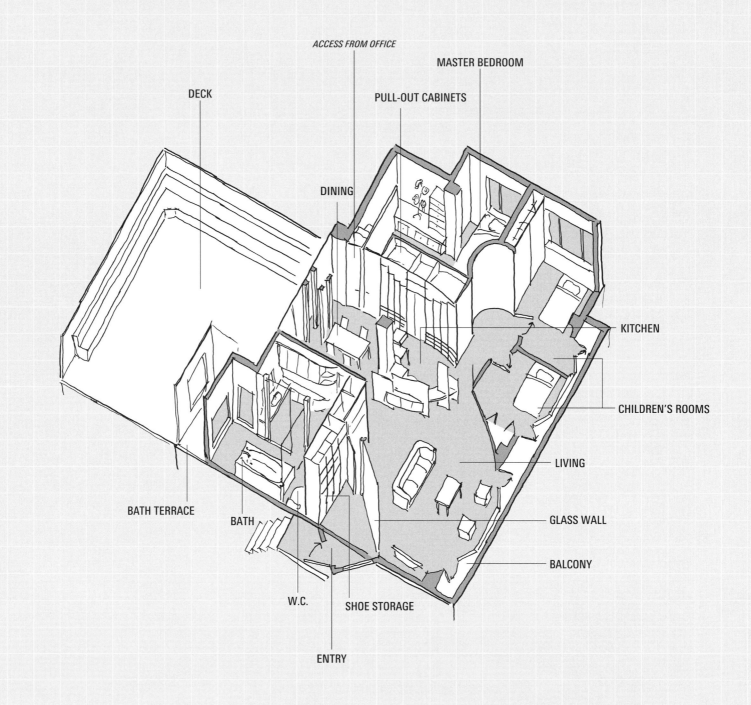

DECK

ACCESS FROM OFFICE

MASTER BEDROOM

PULL-OUT CABINETS

DINING

KITCHEN

CHILDREN'S ROOMS

LIVING

BATH TERRACE

BATH

GLASS WALL

BALCONY

W.C.

SHOE STORAGE

ENTRY

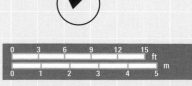

0   3   6   9   12 15
————————————————————— ft
0   1   2   3   4   5
————————————————————— m

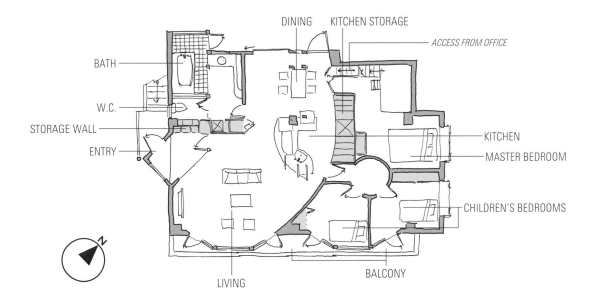

BATH

DINING   KITCHEN STORAGE

ACCESS FROM OFFICE

W.C.

STORAGE WALL

ENTRY

KITCHEN

MASTER BEDROOM

CHILDREN'S BEDROOMS

BALCONY

LIVING

This house differs from others in the book in two important respects. First, it is a renovation, not new construction; second, it is not a freestanding house but more of an apartment, built on the third story of a family-owned business. Still, it has a separate entrance accessible from outside, and the designers, the firm of Pittori Piccoli, approached the design with a free hand, creating an interior whose looseness, comfort, and freshness belie the space's uninspiring origins.

Spread over a single floor, the house is centered on the living room, separated from the entryway by a large glass wall. The boundary with the kitchen is formed by a curved planter that uses hand-cast glass and that forms the back of the kitchen sink and range unit (see detail on page 96). A small dining area is nestled next to a pair of structural columns and has a good view of the large exterior deck. The rear wall of the kitchen is all storage, in beautifully designed pull-out units laid in a broad arc and subdivided to accommodate all of the kitchen storage needs. A similar sense of detailing extends to the illuminated shelving for shoes in the entry, and a storage unit across from the dining table, highlighted by more cast glass.

The gray-tiled bathroom is limited in size but superbly laid out, with large windows that afford a glimpse of the terrace, enclosed by vine-covered trellises for privacy. It is an excellent example of making a space feel larger by giving it a view. A half-height, spring-loaded swinging door to the toilet area provides enough privacy while enhancing ventilation, and also eliminates the cause of a common complaint in houses with children, namely leaving the door open.

The children's bedrooms are configured as a small realm, with a semicircular entrance foyer off the living room large enough for a bench or a computer. The rooms themselves are simple, with large closets and windows. The master bedroom, entered by a narrow door behind the kitchen, is extremely private, and makes use of an existing stairway for extra storage. A small entrance next to the bedroom door gives immediate access to the company offices downstairs.

Pittori Piccoli has devoted considerable attention to varying the vertical heights of the different spaces. In particular, the living room was given a cove treatment with concealed lighting, making the ceiling seem to float, a difficult detail to implement in the existing steel-frame structure, but here carried off seemingly effortlessly. The white floor tiles are durable and brighten the house considerably; the deck is nearly as large as the house itself, and affords ample room for later expansion. All in all, this design is rich and stimulating, with a sensuality in its detailing not often seen in Japanese family homes, a reflection of the taste of the owners (particularly the wife, who oversaw the project), as well as of the innovation and intuition of the designers.

HOUSE IN MOTO-AZABU

Comfortable shelter for a mature couple with cars

DESIGN: Mutsue Hayakusa; Cell Space Architects
CONSTRUCTION: steel frame / 3 floors
OCCUPANTS: couple
LOT: 673 sq. ft. (62.50 sq. m.)
HOUSE: 403 sq. ft. (37.45 sq. m.)
TOTAL FLOOR AREA: 1,209 sq. ft. (112.35 sq. m.)

The narrow entryway flanked by a pair of curving glass walls feels like an auto showroom, a bit of fun for a couple enamored of their cars.

Tough materials are used on the exterior of this urban house for security, but grilles allow light into the interior. The slope of the roof is dictated by sunlight-related building codes.

On the interior, the same sloping roof is sheathed in narrow slats of willow, giving a warm and rhythmic sheltering surface. The third-floor kitchen, with its high ceiling, is light, airy, and well laid out.

A spiral staircase connects the three floors (though a small elevator is included as well); the use of punched metal for the stair treads adds to the overall sense of lightness. The walls of the second-floor bedroom are lined with cabinets, and an easily configurable curved partition can divide the bedroom into separate his and hers areas when desired. (See also detail on page 99.)

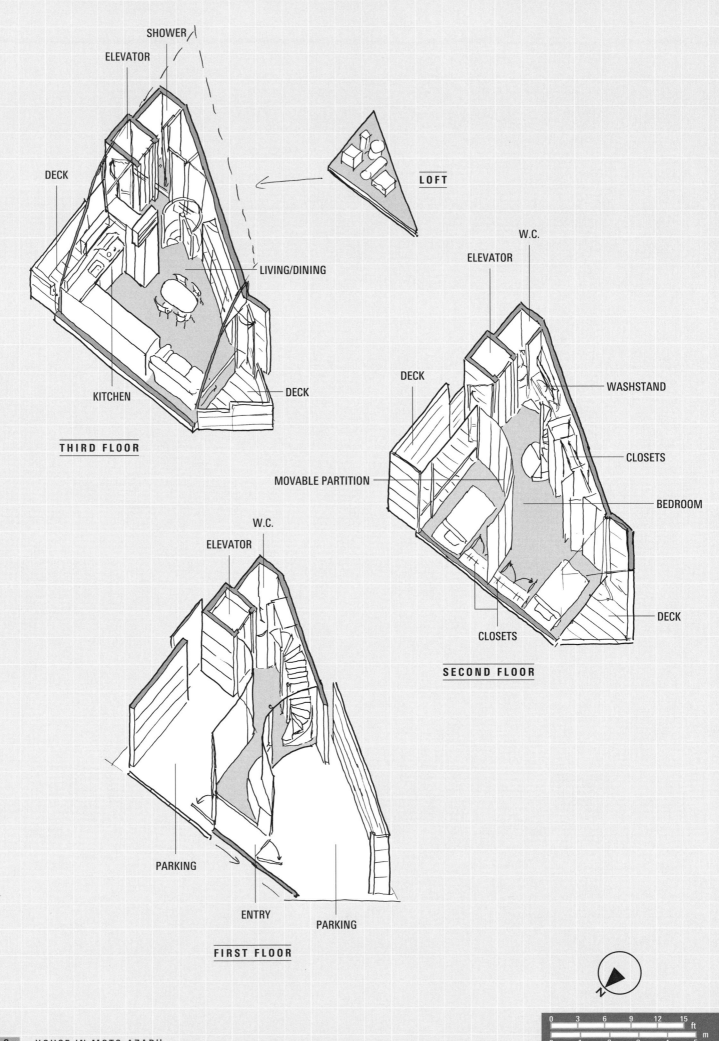

SHOWER

ELEVATOR

DECK

LOFT

LIVING/DINING

KITCHEN

DECK

THIRD FLOOR

W.C.

ELEVATOR

DECK

WASHSTAND

MOVABLE PARTITION

CLOSETS

BEDROOM

CLOSETS

DECK

SECOND FLOOR

W.C.

ELEVATOR

PARKING

ENTRY

PARKING

FIRST FLOOR

N

0   3   6   9   12   15   ft
0   1   2   3   4   5   m

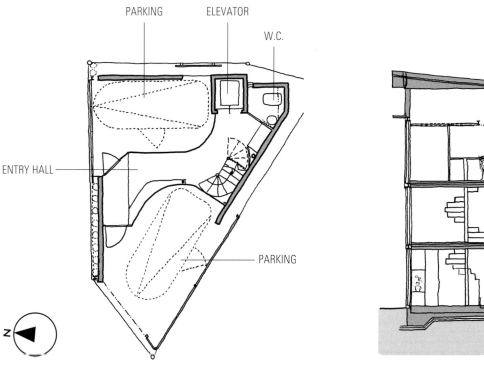

PARKING   ELEVATOR

W.C.

ENTRY HALL

PARKING

N

FIRST FLOOR

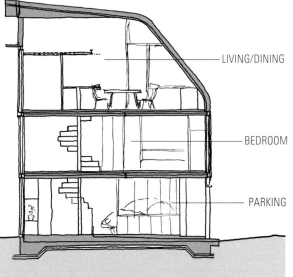

LIVING/DINING

BEDROOM

PARKING

An odd triangular site with strict sunlight requirements dictated the overall shape and size of this three-story home, while the desire for security without sacrificing convenience suggested tough metal exterior materials and wide sliding gates for the entry and driveways. But the fortresslike exterior gives way to a surprising sequence of stimulating, luxurious, and restful interior spaces, beginning with the showroomlike glass-enclosed his and hers parking spaces. A narrow but sweeping spiral staircase seems to float upward, reflected in the mirrorlike stainless steel ceiling, leading through the second-floor bedroom to the lofted living space above. In this sunny space, as well as in the bedroom, one is struck by subtle and unusual coloration, primarily through the use of narrow horizontal slats of golden-green willow as the primary wallcovering. Combined with natural blonde flooring, silklike maroon polyester curtains, and complementary patterned bedcoverings of Thai silk in the bedrooms, the effect is sumptuous and sophisticated.

In the upper space, the living/dining/kitchen area is sheltered and embraced by the rhythmic willow wall, which arches overhead to form the ceiling. Light pours in through full-height windows at the corners. A large sloping wall would ordinarily be a drawback in a living space, but though the one here is primarily the result of building codes that protect the neighbor's access to sunlight, architect Mutsue Hayakusa uses it to lend a dynamic uplift to the room. The result is an invigorating daytime space.

The occupants are a mature couple, and they have found that the house enhances their active lifestyle, and that they receive more than the average number of visits from friends. Hayakusa has utilized an unusually wide color palette, but in an understated manner: pale green walls, bright blue on the interior of a closet (reminiscent of the traditional Japanese aesthetic of lining unprepossessing earthen-hued kimono with brightly colored silks, where they would normally remain unseen).

The second and third floors have mesh-floored corner balconies enclosed in metal grilles that allow illumination into the bedrooms in particular (and would be ideal for potted trees), while the inclusion of an elevator ensures effortless access to all floors. All in all, it is an admirable solution to tough site requirements; the realization of a comfortable and exciting environment for an adventurous mature couple.

HOUSE IN NAKA-IKEGAMI
Sun-filled living on many levels

DESIGN: Tomoyuki Utsumi, Milligram Studio
CONSTRUCTION: wood / 2 floors + loft
OCCUPANTS: family of three
LOT: 623 sq. ft. (57.91 sq. m.)
HOUSE: 374 sq. ft. (34.72 sq. m.)
TOTAL FLOOR AREA: 964 sq. ft. (89.55 sq. m.)

Though actually a three-story home, the Naka-Ikegami House feels like a single open light-filled space. The play of ever-shifting sunlight on white surfaces creates endless drama and makes the home feel like a variety of different spaces.

From the exterior, the house is a tightly sheathed metal-clad box that fills the narrow lot. The sharply sloping roof is angled to draw as much sunlight as possible in through the long skylight.

One wall of the sleeping loft is devoted to storage, which uses every bit of available space.

The owners of the house enjoy cooking, but there was not much room for countertops. The designer hit upon the ingenious idea of making a sturdy pull-out work surface.

The designer has defined the space mainly through the use of levels; the living/dining area opens full height to the ceiling, while the kitchen has both a higher floor and a lower ceiling. The sleeping loft is tucked away above in a manner that makes it more part of the living space than a separate room.

Raised levels often allow for extra underfloor storage space. Here, infrequently used kitchen and dining items are tucked away under the kitchen floor.

The loft itself is cozy and sheltered, yet open, with room for a floor-mounted double bed and not much else, although a large set of closets and cabinets fills one wall (see facing page).

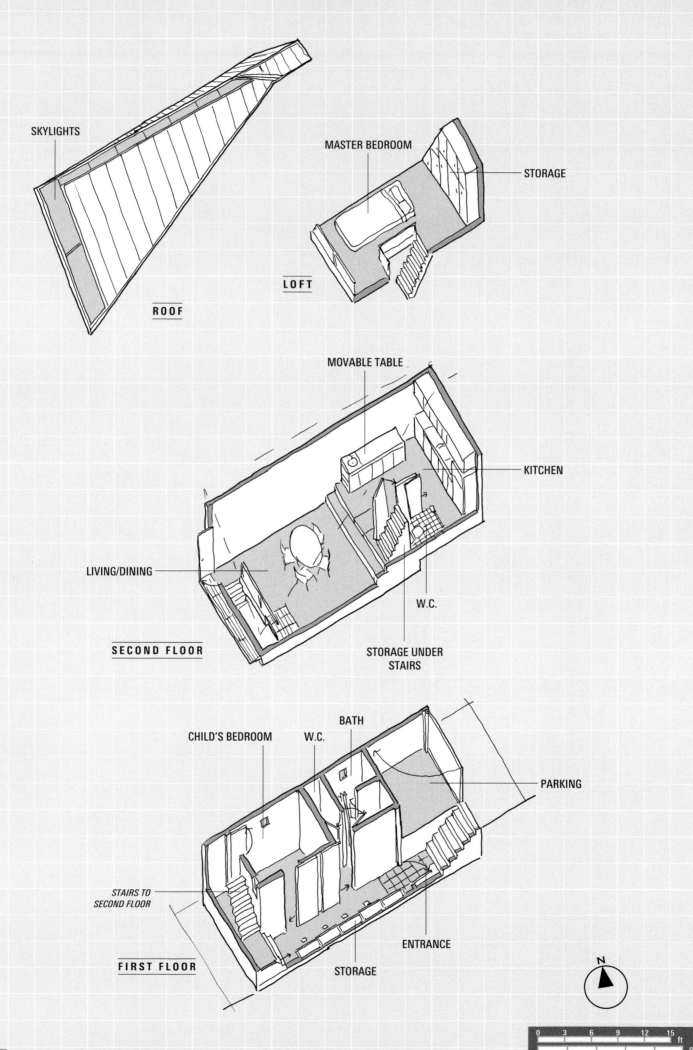

SKYLIGHTS

ROOF

MASTER BEDROOM

STORAGE

LOFT

MOVABLE TABLE

KITCHEN

LIVING/DINING

W.C.

SECOND FLOOR

STORAGE UNDER
STAIRS

CHILD'S BEDROOM

W.C.

BATH

PARKING

STAIRS TO
SECOND FLOOR

FIRST FLOOR

STORAGE

ENTRANCE

N

0   3   6   9   12 15
ft

0   1   2   3   4   5
m

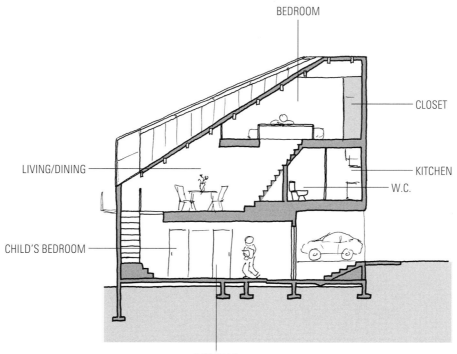

BEDROOM

CLOSET

LIVING/DINING

KITCHEN

W.C.

CHILD'S BEDROOM

BATH/W.C.

A narrow lot hemmed in on all sides by existing buildings presents one of the biggest home design challenges. It is difficult to place windows in the side walls and maintain privacy, so how can one provide natural light? Building upward can maximize usable space, but often results in narrow, boxy proportions. This is why architect Tomoyuki Utsumi's house for a couple with a child is such a pleasant surprise. Utsumi performed a kind of sculptural jujitsu, slicing what otherwise would have been a three-story box at a sharp angle, creating a steeply sloping roof that lends the house a strong character on the exterior and interesting structural dynamics inside. A long skylight climbs from the roof's lowest corner, where it functions as an eye-level window, to the peak, becoming a long gap through which ever-shifting daylight spills.

This is a fun house, in which a dramatic and well-lit ground-floor entry corridor lined with storage leads to a large living space above. Essentially one big room, the living/dining/kitchen area is split by a generous change of level, creating an opportunity for underfloor storage, while the master bedroom is an open loft nestled into the highest corner. An ingenious kitchen cabinet transforms into a table on casters, doubling the available countertop area and making gourmet cooking a realistic option. The bedroom loft features an entire wall of cabinets and closets, and additional storage has been fitted under the stairs, reached by a door that is more like a movable wall.

In this house, achieving adequate headroom in a few particular locations has required some ingenuity. In the loft, for instance, the sloping roof forms the walls, and rather than fight this limitation, the mattress sits low to the floor, futonlike, and the space has been made one for sitting and is quite comfortable that way. At one point on the stairway leading up from the entry, the framing of a typical floor would have given inadequate clearance overhead, so the designer replaced it with a thinner steel grille, which allows in extra illumination as well.

Not that the house is without compromises. The ground-floor bath and the child's bedroom, which don't benefit from the skylight, are fairly dark without artificial light. But the designer and the clients reasoned that since these rooms would be used primarily in the evening the lack of sunlight would be acceptable.

HOUSE IN UMEGAOKA

Central staircase makes movement fun

DESIGN: Mitsuhiko Sato
CONSTRUCTION: reinforced concrete & steel frame / 2 floors + basement
OCCUPANTS: family of three
LOT: 840 sq. ft. (78.0 sq. m.)
HOUSE: 321 sq. ft. (29.81 sq. m.)
TOTAL FLOOR AREA: 963 sq. ft. (89.43 sq. m.)

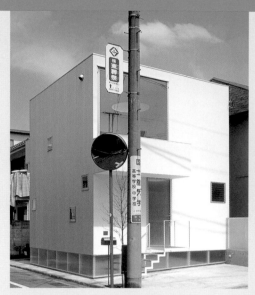

The nearly cubical house is set atop a wrap-around band of glass which brings light into the lowermost floor. A large balcony window also illuminates the second-floor living room.

The first-floor entry corridor is narrow but brightened by a polycarbonate entry door at one end and a floor-to-ceiling window at the other.

This three-story house is designed around a central spiral staircase housed inside a steel cylinder, which also acts as a structural support for the floors. Positioned directly beneath a large circular skylight, it also serves as a light well for the lower floors.

The high-ceilinged living/dining/kitchen provides a comfortable main space for family life. All storage and kitchen accommodations are arrayed along one wall, leaving the others free of obstruction and facilitating the easy arrangement of furniture.

The wrap-around transom windows of the semi-basement make it the best-illuminated room in the house. In addition to housing the bathroom, it is used as a music room and for arts and crafts.

The storage wall in the living/dining/kitchen has cabinets in a variety of sizes and configurations, and ingeniously manages to house both laundry and kitchen facilities as well as miscellany. (See also detail on page 95.)

The master bedroom is divided into a storage and dressing area and a sleeping platform, with the outer wall of the stairwell (*right*), sheathed in matching wood veneer, acting as a natural partition. The space beneath the platform is devoted to storage. (See also detail on page 101.)

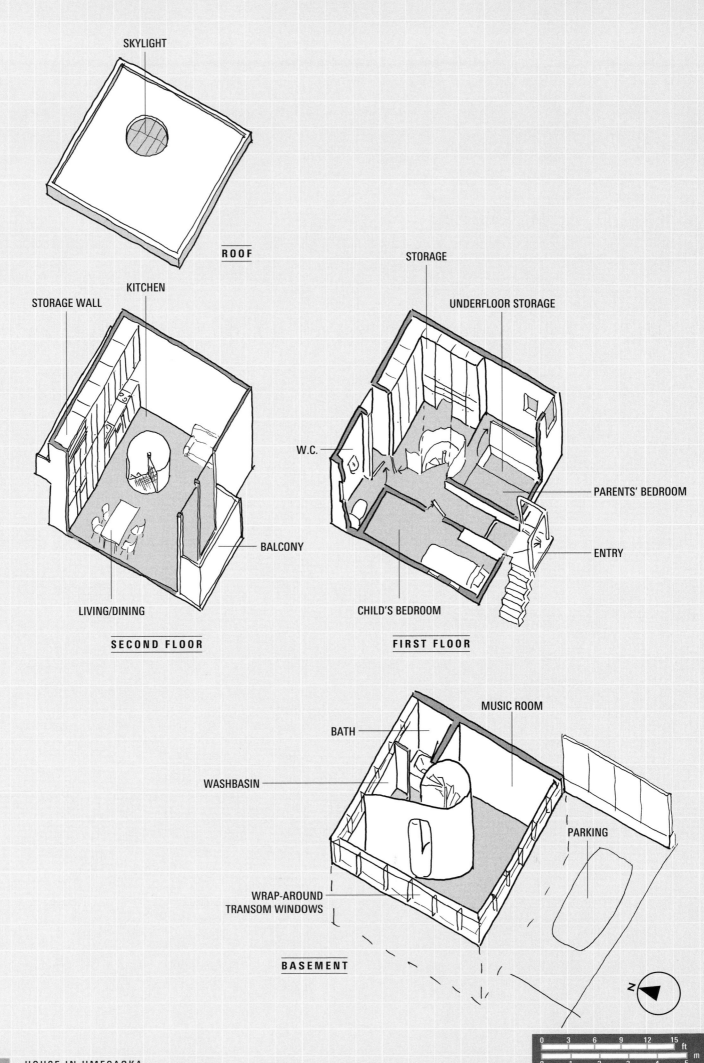

SKYLIGHT

ROOF

STORAGE WALL

KITCHEN

STORAGE

UNDERFLOOR STORAGE

W.C.

PARENTS' BEDROOM

BALCONY

ENTRY

LIVING/DINING

CHILD'S BEDROOM

SECOND FLOOR

FIRST FLOOR

MUSIC ROOM

BATH

WASHBASIN

PARKING

WRAP-AROUND
TRANSOM WINDOWS

BASEMENT

N

0 3 6 9 12 15 ft
0 1 2 3 4 5 m

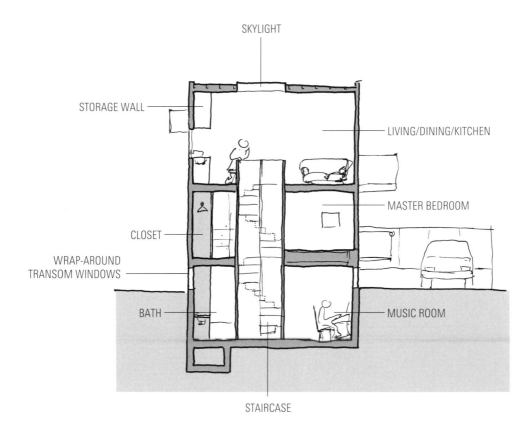

SKYLIGHT

STORAGE WALL

LIVING/DINING/KITCHEN

MASTER BEDROOM

CLOSET

WRAP-AROUND
TRANSOM WINDOWS

BATH

MUSIC ROOM

STAIRCASE

The big idea in this suburban house was to place an expansive, high-ceilinged, and well-lit living/dining/kitchen area on the upper floor where it would receive the most light, locate the bath and a large music room in what might be described as a three-quarters basement, leaving the ground floor for two bedrooms. The use of a steel-frame structure allowed wrap-around transom windows for the below-ground rooms, and the resulting effect, especially at night, is of a two-story cube hovering above the ground. The architect's other brainstorm was to use a steel culvert 5 feet (1.5 m.) in diameter as both a structural element and enclosure for a spiral staircase running from the cellar to the upper floor. Painted white, filled with steel mesh stair treads, and aligned with a matching circular skylight, it brings additional light into the lower stories.

The living room is totally unobstructed, and features a massive line of storage cabinets housing everything from kitchen appliances to laundry equipment, including a clever pop-out ironing board (see detail on page 95). Wood floors and ceiling lend the living space warmth, and large sliding doors open onto a cozy balcony overlooking the entryway below. The ground floor is neatly bisected by the narrow entry corridor, with the child's bedroom to the left, and an extremely well-conceived master bedroom to the right. This bedroom is again divided roughly in half by the curved wall of the staircase, and includes two walls formed by elegant cabinets as well as generous underfloor storage (made feasible by the use of futons for bedding).

The clear zoning of the house—in which living, sleeping, and musical recreation are confined to different floors—would seem to have drawbacks for a family with children. But thanks to the nearly magical storage wall, the generous living space fulfills the many needs of daily life with aplomb, and allows the family to be together most of the day.

When family members want to sequester themselves in the basement to think musical thoughts, the size and placement of the staircase provide a feeling of immediate connection to the rest of the house; it is a straight-line conduit for light as well as communication.

PENGUIN HOUSE
Living in the treetops

DESIGN: Yasuhiro Yamashita, Atelier Tekuto; Masahiro Ikeda, Mias
CONSTRUCTION: steel frame / 3 floors
OCCUPANTS: couple
LOT: 549 sq. ft. (50.99 sq. m.)
HOUSE: 332 sq. ft. (30.80 sq. m.)
TOTAL FLOOR AREA: 899 sq. ft. (83.56 sq. m.)

The exterior appearance of the house is primarily established by the thin curved steel panels that make up the main structure. The living/dining/kitchen is perched above like a crow's nest, and corner indentations are fitted with windows on all sides.

The kitchen corner on the third floor makes use of a tiny bit of open space above the stairwell for the range.

The site is surrounded by trees, and the surrounding glass walls of the third floor give the sense of living in the treetops.

The second-floor bedroom is light and ethereal, and provides an unexpected sense of privacy. The closet is enclosed by a gauzy curtain on the right, behind which light spills downward from the upper floor.

The bath is tucked into a rear corner of the house where it benefits from a tall corner window. Curtains are used to divide the tub, shower, and washbasin areas. (See also detail on page 108.)

The stairway is a simple straight run of open stairs, climbing toward the light.

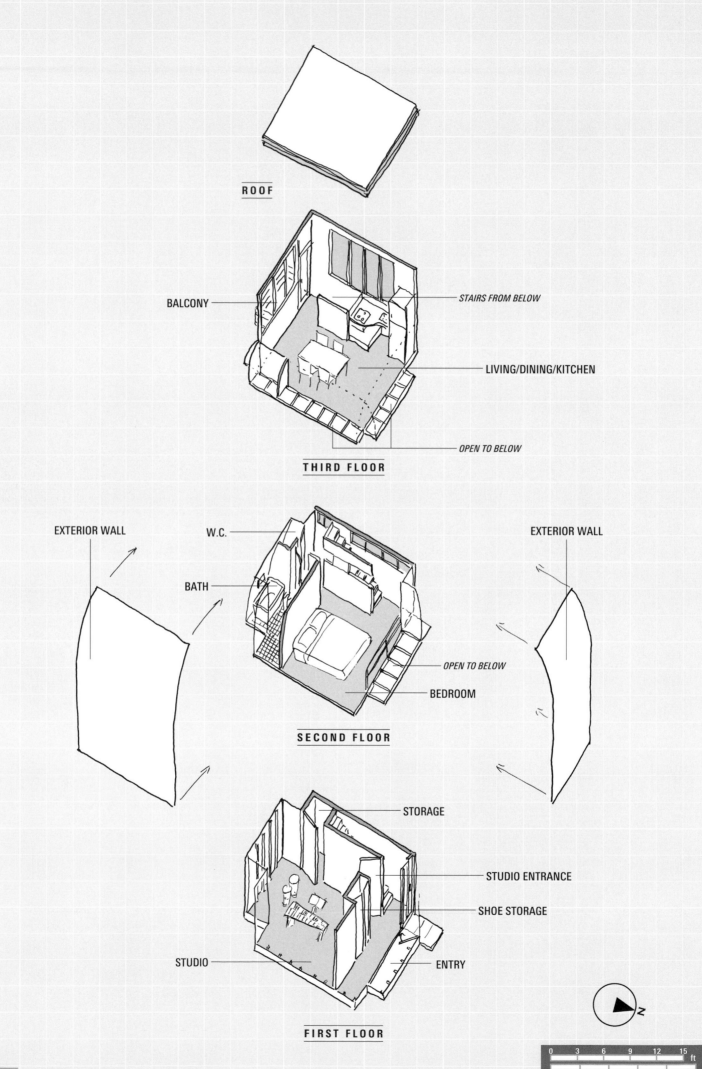

ROOF

BALCONY — STAIRS FROM BELOW

LIVING/DINING/KITCHEN

OPEN TO BELOW

THIRD FLOOR

EXTERIOR WALL

W.C.

BATH

EXTERIOR WALL

OPEN TO BELOW

BEDROOM

SECOND FLOOR

STORAGE

STUDIO ENTRANCE

SHOE STORAGE

STUDIO — ENTRY

FIRST FLOOR

0 3 6 9 12 15 ft
0 1 2 3 4 5 m

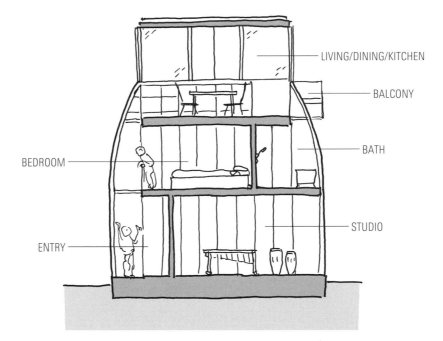

LIVING/DINING/KITCHEN

BALCONY

BATH

BEDROOM

STUDIO

ENTRY

This three-story home with a small 550-square-foot (51-sq.-m.) footprint owes its radical appearance to a convergence of factors: fortuitous location aside the tree-lined approach to a shrine, the less-fortunate necessity of having to build on a site that was formerly a two-car driveway, an extremely constrained budget, and clients whose sense of adventure neatly parallels that of their architect. The main theme of the house could be summed up as "life in the treetops," and indeed the glass-enclosed third-floor space (living/dining/kitchen) gives that sense. In contrast, the ground floor is devoted to the owners' fully soundproofed percussion studio, and the second floor houses a single bedroom—surprisingly bright, airy, and ethereal—and the bathroom. A simple run of stairs links the three floors.

Which brings us to the structure: arched 1/8-inch (3.2-mm) steel panels stiffened by vertical steel ribs, painted with 1/16-inch-thick (1.6-mm) coats of special high-performance insulating aerospace epoxy. Engineer Masahiro Ikeda, widely sought after by Japanese architects attempting the improbable, found a secure, code-satisfying structural solution to realize the architect's brainstorm. In pursuit of lower costs, using less building material became a primary goal. One property of steel sheets is that they become stronger and more rigid if they are flexed, so lightweight, thin sheets can provide quite enough strength. Add several vertical ribs, even lightweight ones, and an extremely strong and secure building panel can be made. Punching holes through a panel like this for windows, however, would seriously weaken it, so the designers decided to light the lower floors by leaving tall gaps at the corners that could be filled with glass. In addition, gaps have been left between the upper floors and the exterior wall, connected with short steel struts, enhancing air circulation and allowing light to play upward and downward.

Moving through this house is like moving through three different worlds. The ground-floor music studio is solid and inwardly focused. Well enclosed, it nevertheless affords pedestrians outside a peek at rehearsals when the corner curtains are opened. With light spilling in at the corners and from the edge of the floor and ceiling, the second-floor bedroom feels like it is floating but is somehow extremely private. Finally, the cupola-like upper living space is invigorating and liberating, allowing one to feel like the master of the domain outside. The owners, not surprisingly, are in love with the house and take every opportunity to share their special lifestyle with visitors.

GLASS SHUTTER HOUSE
Disappearing walls and an airy atrium

DESIGN: Shigeru Ban Architects
CONSTRUCTION: steel frame / 3 floors
OCCUPANTS: family of three
LOT: 1,430 sq. ft. (132.89 sq. m.)
HOUSE: 814 sq. ft. (75.65 sq. m.)
TOTAL FLOOR AREA: 1,624 sq. ft. (150.85 sq. m.)

With the shutters closed the house is a trim box. An open terrace on the side of the house provides parking and direct access to the living spaces, but can also be used for restaurant seating. The large overhang houses shutters when that portion is open.

The restaurant is a well appointed, chic but casual space that features a large glassed-in refrigerator used as a display case.

The second-floor kitchen of the house itself makes use of an island, and can be used for videotaping cooking shows.

Simple in form but radical in concept, the Glass Shutter House can open two of its faces entirely to the elements. The ground floor houses a restaurant, and the living spaces on the second and third floors are stepped back, forming a large atrium.

The view from the third floor gives a sense of just how open the house is, more like series of outdoor terraces than a conventional home.

Tall curtains provide another layer of closure, and blow in the breeze in a way that activates the entire house.

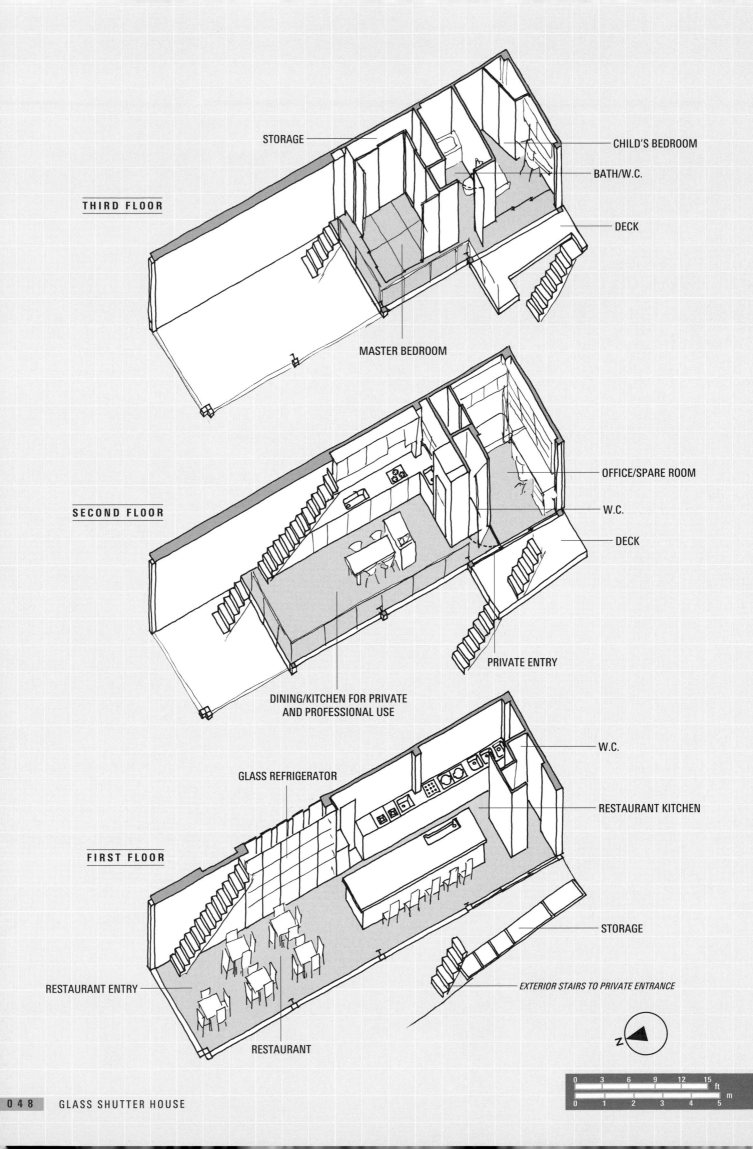

THIRD FLOOR

STORAGE

CHILD'S BEDROOM

BATH/W.C.

DECK

MASTER BEDROOM

SECOND FLOOR

OFFICE/SPARE ROOM

W.C.

DECK

PRIVATE ENTRY

DINING/KITCHEN FOR PRIVATE
AND PROFESSIONAL USE

GLASS REFRIGERATOR

W.C.

RESTAURANT KITCHEN

FIRST FLOOR

STORAGE

RESTAURANT ENTRY

EXTERIOR STAIRS TO PRIVATE ENTRANCE

RESTAURANT

0 3 6 9 12 15
ft
0 1 2 3 4 5
m

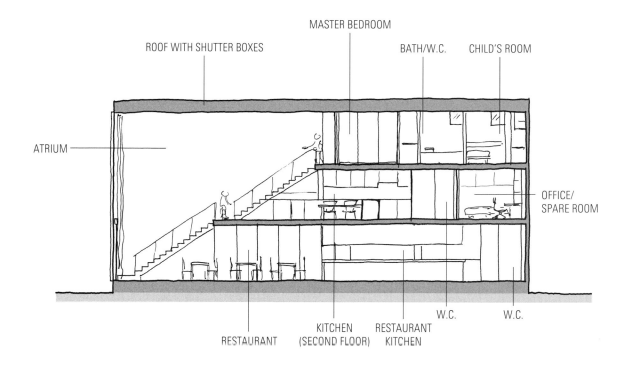

ROOF WITH SHUTTER BOXES

MASTER BEDROOM

BATH/W.C.　CHILD'S ROOM

ATRIUM

OFFICE/
SPARE ROOM

RESTAURANT

KITCHEN
(SECOND FLOOR)

RESTAURANT
KITCHEN

W.C.　　　W.C.

Architect Shigeru Ban is known for innovative structural ideas that seek to liberate interior space, often achieving seemingly impossibly wide vistas in tight residential quarters. In this case, the client is a well-known chef who wanted to live above his restaurant, and who also needed to be able to use his kitchen for on-air demonstrations. Commercial decisions largely guided the choice of site, which is on a heavily traveled and densely built suburban shopping street, and both the architect and client agreed that opening the restaurant fully to the street was an exciting idea. Ban's solution was to stack the residential spaces—a dining area, kitchen/living room, and office on the second floor and bedrooms and bath on the third—above the 815-square-foot (76-sq.-m.) first-floor restaurant, with each floor receding to form a three-story atrium that widens as it rises.

The house occupies a bit more than half of the site, the rest having been left open for parking and a terrace. Ban saw the opportunity to open both the narrow street front and the wall facing the terrace by means of three-story-high retractable glass shutters, like upscale garage doors, and tall curtains. The result is a fantastic openness and a beautiful play of light and breeze throughout the house. The residents are able to look down from the living spaces as well as outward and upward, and the actual act of opening the shutters creates a sense of drama. Ban solved the circulation problems simply and straightforwardly: two runs of stairs, one inside, one out. The indoor stairs provide the residents with access to the living quarters above, and are the primary link between the living and sleeping areas. The exterior stairs are a means of bypassing the restaurant to reach the second-floor entryway of the house itself, in addition to leading to a kind of sky terrace on the third floor which affords a stunning vista of the surrounding cityscape.

Houses are always an expression of priorities, and here it is clear that the restaurant space is the most important area, and the expansive second-floor kitchen the second. In contrast, the bedrooms—a tatami-floored Japanese-style master bedroom and a smaller one for the couple's daughter—are reasonably minimal, though they benefit immensely from the vistas they command. The house as a whole is a showpiece, and on pleasant evenings with the ethereal curtains floating in the breeze the effect is otherworldly and magical.

T-SET HOUSE
Snug, sunny space for a couple

DESIGN: Chiba Manabu Architects
CONSTRUCTION: wood / 2 floors + mezzanine
OCCUPANTS: young couple
LOT: 679 sq. ft. (63.05 sq. m.), with parking
HOUSE: 339 sq. ft. (31.52 sq. m.)
TOTAL FLOOR AREA: 618 sq. ft. (57.42 sq. m.)

T-set is actually a pair of houses snuggled together on a small lot. The smaller of the two is a speculative property tucked behind the owners' house, its entrance visible here to the left.

The architect paid careful attention to the size and placement of windows, to maximize both light and privacy. The upstairs bedroom, seen here, uses movable partitions, and faces a narrow light well which opens to the living room below. (See also detail on page 102.)

The living room is a large volume, with a tunnel-like entry corridor to the right. The kitchen and bath are housed in a compact black box alongside which stairs are located.

Above the kitchen is a small mezzanine for comfortable seating. Stairs to the left lead up to the bedrooms

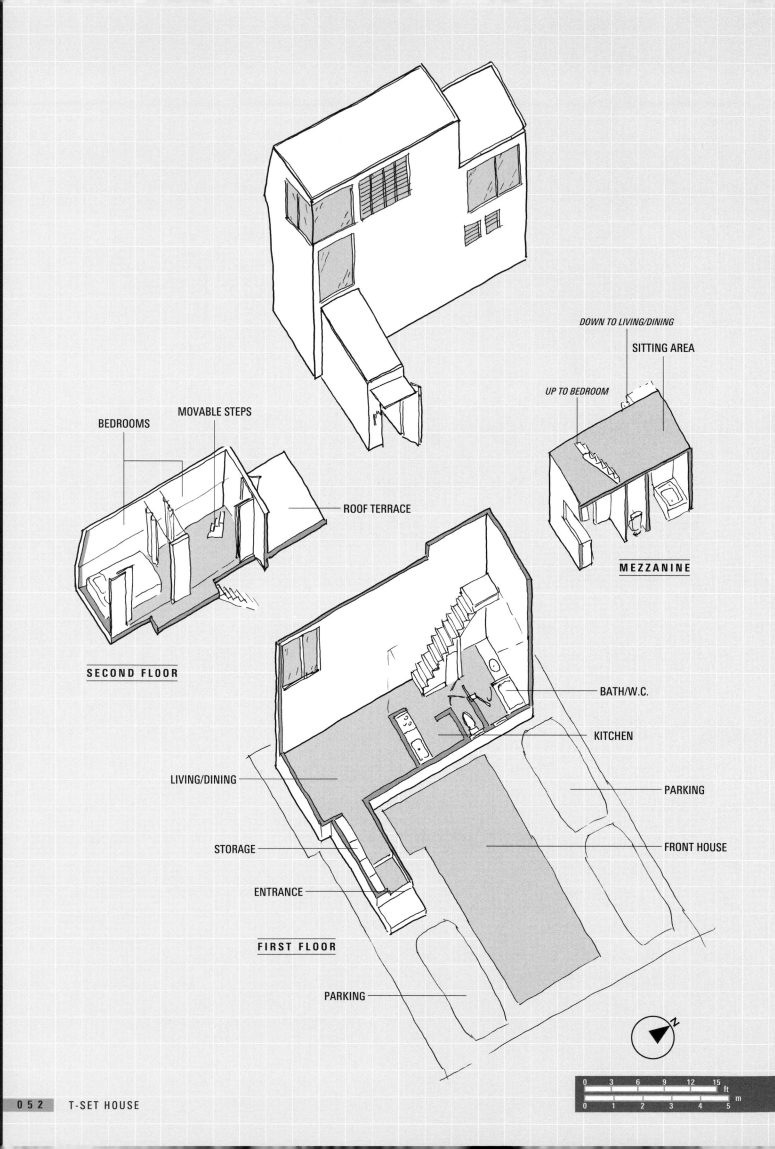

DOWN TO LIVING/DINING

SITTING AREA

UP TO BEDROOM

BEDROOMS

MOVABLE STEPS

ROOF TERRACE

MEZZANINE

SECOND FLOOR

BATH/W.C.

KITCHEN

LIVING/DINING

PARKING

STORAGE

FRONT HOUSE

ENTRANCE

FIRST FLOOR

PARKING

0 3 6 9 12 15 ft

0 1 2 3 4 5 m

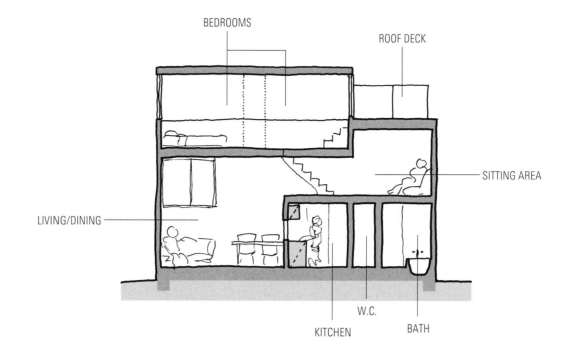

BEDROOMS

ROOF DECK

SITTING AREA

LIVING/DINING

W.C.

KITCHEN

BATH

When approached by a developer to build two houses on a 1,515-square-foot (140-sq.-m.) lot in a dense section of Tokyo, architect Manabu Chiba immediately rejected the suggestion of placing them side by side. One house was to become the owners' residence, the other a speculative property, and Chiba put great thought into how best to give them distinct identities, maintain privacy, and maximize natural illumination. He eventually arrived at a T-shaped arrangement that placed the houses in close proximity—less than a yard apart—but which allowed him to coordinate their parking, entrances, and window openings to achieve his goals. (The owners' house at the front of the lot will not be discussed due to privacy considerations.)

Sold shortly after completion, the rear house has a total floor space of 620 square feet (57 sq. m.), and has two stories with a kind of mid-level mezzanine as well as an exterior roof terrace. The house is approached through the parking space and entered through a long tunnel-like corridor that has storage along one wall. The transition to the high-ceilinged, light-filled living/dining room is almost explosive. Chiba has organized the interior of this house by considering it a large, white, unified volume into which two smaller black volumes have been nested. A rectangular volume on the ground floor contains the kitchen, bath, and lavatory. A small opening acts as a countertop and pass-through from the kitchen to the dining area. The top of this volume, reached by a simple run of stairs, is a quiet sitting area whose large window overlooks the neighbor's parking space but which nevertheless feels very private. Another short flight of stairs leads to another black volume, which seems to float overhead and contains the bedrooms. Brilliantly illuminated by a large window which, thanks to a small atrium arrangement, also serves the living area downstairs, the bedroom area feels like a secure, secluded nest (see detail on page 102). A simple closet consisting of a rod and curtains on both sides separates the two sleeping areas and the whole is easily sealed off by sliding doors. Finally, the roof terrace is accessed by a short set of steps on casters that can be moved out of the way when not needed, freeing up more floor space.

This house feels much larger than it is due to Chiba's sense of scale and proportion. He has created several spaces on different levels that have different ceiling heights and quite distinct atmospheres. The stairs, which double back, make an interesting progression through the house and seem to increase the distance from downstairs to upstairs. Finally, Chiba has ingeniously engineered the structure of the house, using various means of suspension and cantilever to make the upper volume appear to float. The house feels expansive, open, and private, and nestles snugly together with the front home while seeming to be unaffected by its presence.

SORA NO KATACHI HOUSE
Scale and materials shape an updated tradition

DESIGN: Kazuhiko Kishimoto, Atelier Cinqu
CONSTRUCTION: wood / 2 floors + basement
OCCUPANTS: family of three
LOT: 810 sq. ft. (75.2 sq. m.)
HOUSE: 448 sq. ft. (41.6 sq. m.)
TOTAL FLOOR AREA: 911 sq. ft. (84.6 sq. m.)

On the exterior, the house appears to be a simple cubic volume. Sculptural projections and slatted panels hint at floor levels and window placement within.

TOP: The garden is actually only a few meters across, but adds a great feeling of depth.

BOTTOM: The living room is split into two levels. The upper level looks out over attractive beams and has a comfortable seating area.

The house is laid out around a garden, and features views across and diagonally from room to room.

The second floor corridor widens into a deck next to the child's room. One side overlooks the garden, and the other has translucent fabric screening which can also be illuminated at night.

The lower half of the living room is designed for floor-level seating, particularly for dining. Large *shoji*-screened windows open it up both to the street and the garden. (See also detail on page 103.)

The house makes use of traditional exterior corridors, connecting the dining/kitchen with the bath and master bedroom on the ground floor.

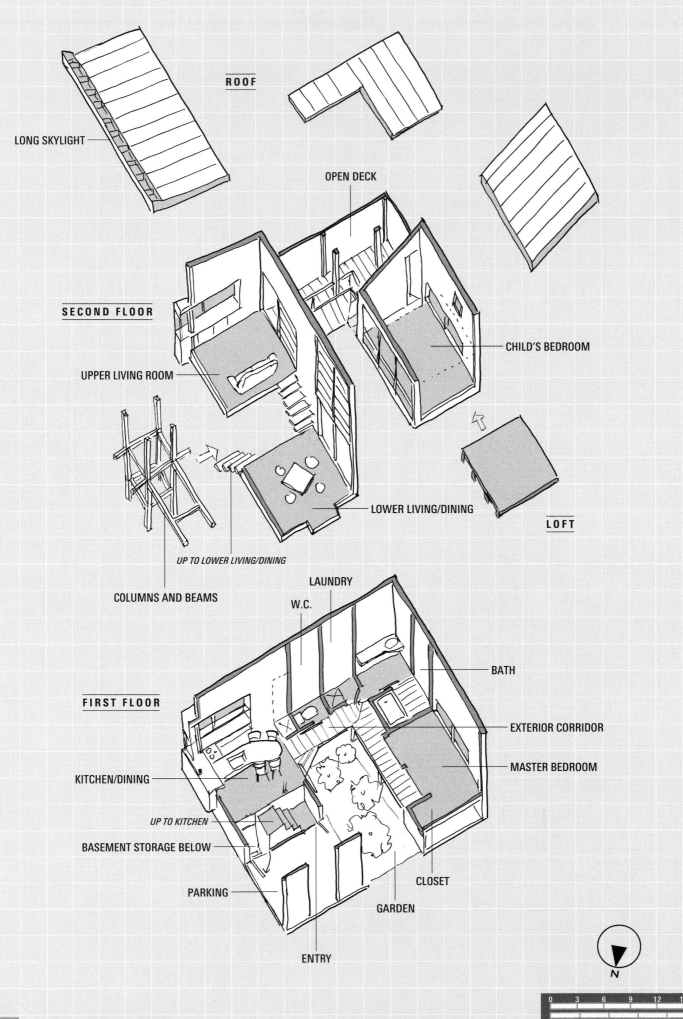

ROOF

LONG SKYLIGHT

OPEN DECK

SECOND FLOOR

UPPER LIVING ROOM

CHILD'S BEDROOM

LOWER LIVING/DINING

LOFT

UP TO LOWER LIVING/DINING

COLUMNS AND BEAMS

LAUNDRY

W.C.

BATH

FIRST FLOOR

EXTERIOR CORRIDOR

MASTER BEDROOM

KITCHEN/DINING

UP TO KITCHEN

BASEMENT STORAGE BELOW

CLOSET

PARKING

GARDEN

ENTRY

N

0   3   6   9   12   15 ft
0   1   2   3   4   5 m

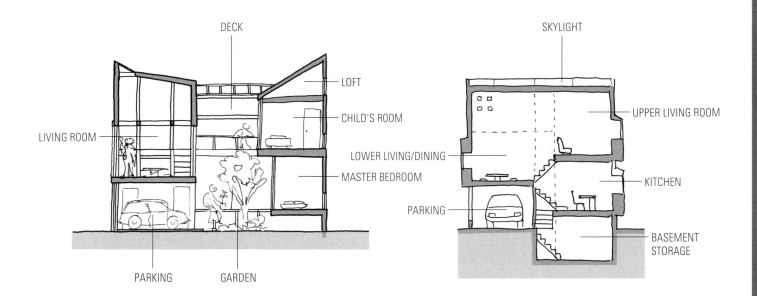

The Japanese name of this house means "shape of the sky," and refers to the fact that the sky above the garden is visible from every room. Architect Kazuhiko Kishimoto built the house for himself and his family. Two stories high with a basement for storage, it exhibits an exquisite sense of scale, is full of handmade details and natural materials, and subtly demonstrates the designer's sophisticated and modern sense of spatial development coupled with an appreciation of the best aspects of traditional Japanese houses. It is also a very personalized space, a work of poetry.

Wrapped around an intimate and beautifully designed central garden, the house is divided into wings linked by exterior verandas, a traditional feature rarely seen today. The main wing, which is entered by stepping up into a small kitchen with a cozy counter and subtle lighting reminiscent of tiny Japanese coffee shops, has a living room on the second floor, while a two-story bedroom wing lies on the opposite side of the garden, linked by verandas on both stories. The circulation is contrived so that the parents' bedroom is at the end of one route, and the child's at the end of another — psychologically separate, but in fact stacked vertically.

The adventurous circulation through the house gives the sense that one is progressing through many different spaces, and as in the best traditional Japanese houses, new vistas constantly open up. The scale of the interior spaces varies from a two-story atrium in the living room to a narrow corridor whose ceiling is low enough to touch; there are constant changes of direction and no fewer than seven distinct floor levels, but Kishimoto has deployed them in a masterful way that feels absolutely natural and appropriate.

Every space opens onto the garden, and the passage of the sun creates a constantly shifting highlight that suggests where to sit. Kishimoto has created many kinds of spaces, enclosed in a variety of ways, grouping them naturally, often without setting clear boundaries. There is ample outdoor space, for instance, and the second-floor veranda, which is walled in translucent fabric and feels very private, widens into a generous deck adjacent to the lofted child's room, creating a distinct child's realm. Similarly, the living room is a dramatic, top-lit, split-level space connected by a short run of steps. The lower half can easily be used for floor-seated dining, and the upper portion forms an overlooking balcony with a couch and corner window, the builder's preferred spot for listening to music. The two levels are connected but separate, and it is easy to imagine conversation flowing back and forth. This is the dramatic heart of the house, with exposed posts and beams, contrasting white and black walls, and large windows that can be opened by layered shutters, *shoji* screens, and sliding glass doors, transforming an introspective space into a transparent and open one (see detail on page 103). This house is a small masterpiece, simultaneously modern and traditional, fresh but familiar.

WHITE BOX HOUSE
Elaborate cabinetry makes home sweet

DESIGN: Shigekazu Takayasu & Naoki Soeda, Architecture Lab
CONSTRUCTION: wood / 2 floors
OCCUPANTS: family of three
LOT: 1,655 sq. ft. (153.77 sq. m.)
HOUSE: 559 sq. ft. (51.89 sq. m.)
TOTAL FLOOR AREA: 1,028 sq. ft. (95.48 sq. m.)

The upper floor is essentially a one-room living space. Very well-designed built-in cabinets, cupboards, and nooks (see detail on page 105) have been arranged in a line along the skylit side of the space. The living space itself forms a long wedge that widens toward the large window facing the street; the ceiling slopes upward in the same direction, giving an illusion of greater width.

The exterior appearance of the house gives it its name, White Box. Set back from the street, there is room for parking in front.

◀ One key to the success of this small house is a long skylight and an arrangement of floors that allows natural light to spill down to the lower floor. The stairs here lead directly to the kitchen. (See also details on pages 101 and 103.)

The kitchen is a showcase of compact design. Most functions are accommodated within a narrow skylit, glass-floored corridor, and extensive use is made of wagons, which pull out from under the counter. Extra counter space wraps around on one side (see detail on page 96) and the glass floor acts as a skylight for the lower level.

The bathroom is simply laid out and has a large window that faces a private service alley. The glass wall that divides the bath from the toilet area is an attractive necessity that allows illumination into the small space.

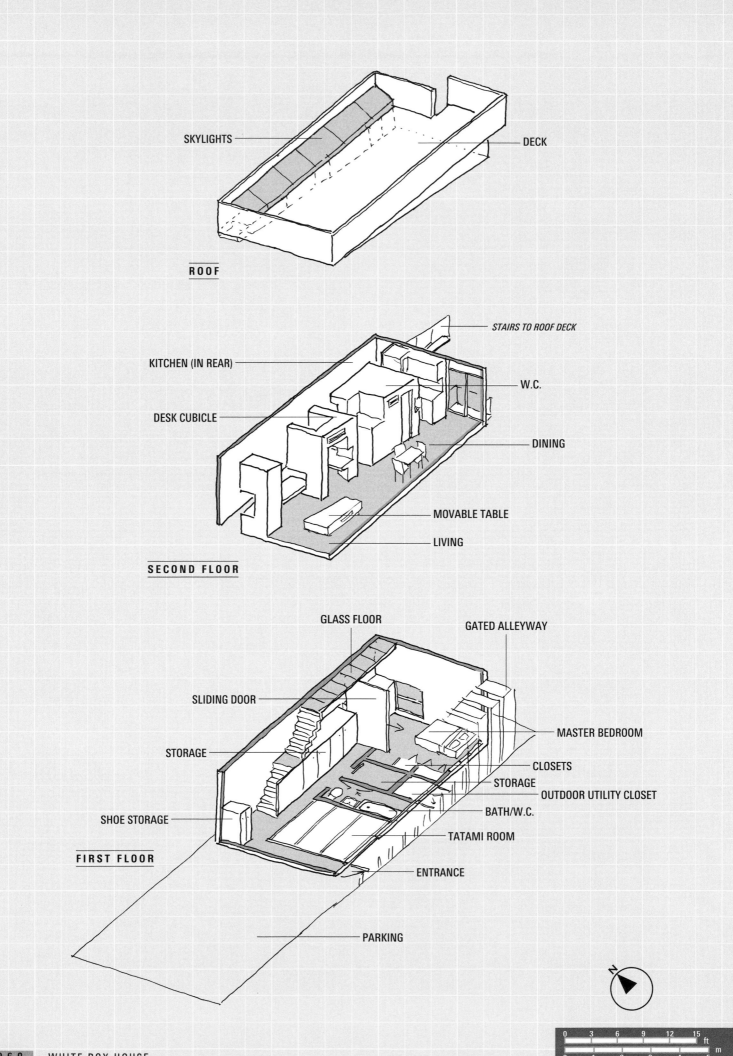

ROOF

SKYLIGHTS

DECK

SECOND FLOOR

STAIRS TO ROOF DECK

KITCHEN (IN REAR)

DESK CUBICLE

W.C.

DINING

MOVABLE TABLE

LIVING

FIRST FLOOR

GLASS FLOOR

GATED ALLEYWAY

SLIDING DOOR

STORAGE

MASTER BEDROOM

CLOSETS

STORAGE

OUTDOOR UTILITY CLOSET

BATH/W.C.

SHOE STORAGE

TATAMI ROOM

ENTRANCE

PARKING

0 3 6 9 12 15 ft
0 1 2 3 4 5 m

SUN IN THE SOUTH

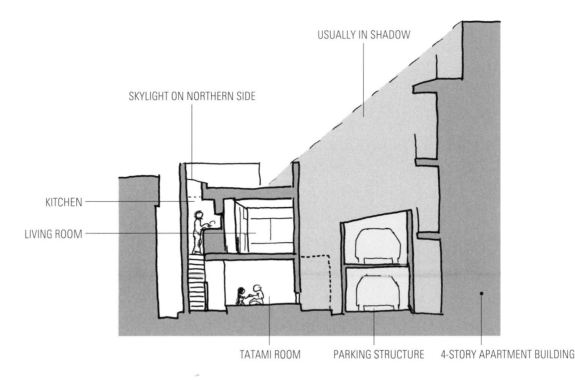

USUALLY IN SHADOW

SKYLIGHT ON NORTHERN SIDE

KITCHEN

LIVING ROOM

TATAMI ROOM   PARKING STRUCTURE   4-STORY APARTMENT BUILDING

Although the exterior form of this house is boxy, the interior is inspired and intricate. Architects Shigekazu Takayasu and Naoki Soeda have graced it with a full complement of features, despite the fact that the two-story woodframe building has a footprint of only 560 square feet (52 sq. m.), and only about a 1,030-square-foot (95-sq.-m.) floor area overall. Particularly interesting is the use of elaborate cabinetry to separate the second-floor living and dining area from the skylit stairway atrium and glass-floored kitchen that occupy one long side of the house. Built at a shallow angle to the main volume of the house, this wall of cabinetry works with a subtly sloping ceiling to create a false sense of perspective, visually elongating the living space. Functioning visually almost like a three-dimensional abstract sculpture, it houses a TV table and stereo cabinet (with a low table on casters that pulls out), an office nook, a washing machine cabinet, a small lavatory, and kitchen storage, as well as the air conditioning system. Light from the shallow atrium beyond spills in through a variety of interesting openings, some high, some low, creating a constant play of shifting light. It is a very inspired feature. (See also details on pages 96, 103, and 105.)

About a third of the ground floor is devoted to storage: a large storage room, a smaller storage room accessed from the outside, closets in the master bedroom, and shelves that extend nearly the full length of the house under the staircase and kitchen. In addition to the master bedroom there is a small tatami-floored room that can be used for guests or eventually as a bedroom for the couple's infant child, and the lavatory/bath. All of the rooms on this floor receive light through windows or sliding glass doors opening onto a securely gated trellised alleyway. Finally, a roof terrace is reached by stairs leading up from the kitchen door.

Considering the disadvantages of the narrow site—set far back from the street, bordered by apartment buildings—the architects did an excellent job of placing the skylights and atrium in the best location for receiving direct sunlight, and of finding ways of bringing the light as deeply into the interior as possible.

AMBI-FLUX HOUSE

When the only way to go is up

DESIGN: Akira Yoneda, Architecton; Masahiro Ikeda, Mias
CONSTRUCTION: steel frame / 5 floors, 3 for living
OCCUPANTS: family of four
LOT: 451 sq. ft. (41.90 sq. m.)
HOUSE: 389 sq. ft. (36.12 sq. m.)
TOTAL FLOOR AREA: 1,735 sq. ft. (161.16 sq. m.)

The narrow-fronted site itself once held a traditional shop-house; from the exterior the house seems to camouflage itself as an office building. Businesses occupy the first two floors.

The roof garden is reached by a final flight of spiral stairs. Bridgelike corridors that span the atrium along one side, like the one that leads to the open master bedroom, are floored in glass to maximize light.

The toplit three-story house is laid out around an atrium with several flights of white, cantilevered stairs. Nylon netting provides security.

The living/dining room is wood floored and features simple matching furnishings, including a suspended shoe cabinet to the left (see also detail on page 104). The kitchen sink is located on an island behind a simple half-height partition, and the rest of the kitchen can be closed away behind folding white doors.

The rooftop garden is a small retreat open to the sky and isolated from the world.

The bedrooms are stacked above each other, the children's below, the parents' above. The children's room in particular is designed for flexibility, with moveable cabinet-partitions. Both bedrooms gain light from the translucent glass wall at the front of the house.

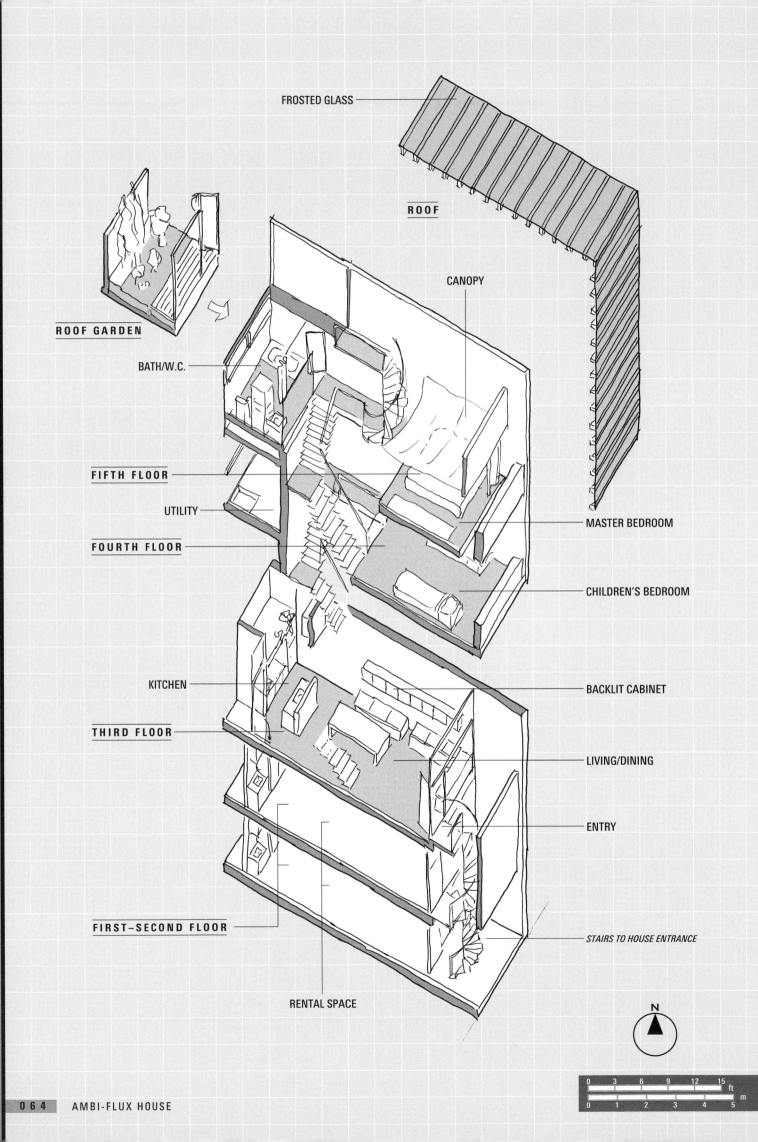

FROSTED GLASS

ROOF

CANOPY

ROOF GARDEN

BATH/W.C.

FIFTH FLOOR

MASTER BEDROOM

UTILITY

FOURTH FLOOR

CHILDREN'S BEDROOM

KITCHEN

BACKLIT CABINET

THIRD FLOOR

LIVING/DINING

ENTRY

FIRST−SECOND FLOOR

STAIRS TO HOUSE ENTRANCE

RENTAL SPACE

N

| 0 | 3 | 6 | 9 | 12 | 15 |
ft
| 0 | 1 | 2 | 3 | 4 | 5 |
m

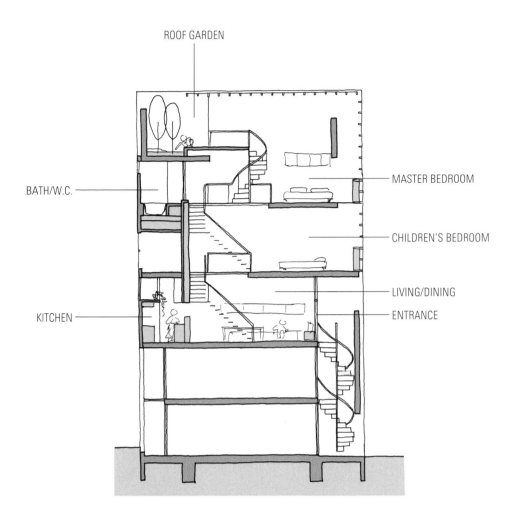

ROOF GARDEN

BATH/W.C.

KITCHEN

MASTER BEDROOM

CHILDREN'S BEDROOM

LIVING/DINING

ENTRANCE

The owners of this house were faced with a dilemma: was it worth demolishing the family's traditional but worn out two-story shop/house and attempting to cope with what had become a very dense and primarily commercial urban area, or should they move to the suburbs? The answer came in the form of a very assertive but extremely inward-looking house with shops on the lower floors, an unusually tall house that camouflages itself as a pencil-thin office building. Atop two stories of rental space is perched what is in effect a three-story townhouse with an intimate, sheltered roof garden. A vast central atrium crowned by a translucent roof creates a tremendous sense of upward expansion, and stairs impart motion and drama. All the interior surfaces are either white, translucent, or of warm natural wood, with exterior views carefully framed to maintain the family's privacy.

The house is entered by means of a shielded, external steel spiral staircase, which opens onto the primary living space, a 310-square-foot (29-sq.-m.) living/dining/kitchen. Flights of white stairs cantilevered from the walls lead upward, first to the children's room, and then further to the master bedroom, both of which are open to deep atriumlike balconies. A small bathroom occupies the rear of the house on the master bedroom level. A steel spiral staircase leads to the roof garden. If all those stairs sound daunting, well, they're also exciting; the children seem to love racing endlessly up and down. What the designer has done is devise a vertical circulation that suits the family's daily cycle: most of the day is spent on the lowermost (third) floor, with the children spending some time playing in their shared bedroom; the parents' bedroom and the bath are primarily nighttime spaces. The owners do not envision occupying the house as it is until their old age, but have worked out a plan for modifying and re-dividing the entire building as their daughters grow up, marry, and the next generation takes over.

NATURAL WEDGE HOUSE
Stark geometry suffused with light

DESIGN: Masaki Endoh; Endoh Design House; Masahiro Ikeda, Mias
CONSTRUCTION: steel frame / 3 floors + basement
OCCUPANTS: young couple
LOT: 625 sq. ft. (58.05 sq. m.)
HOUSE: 372 sq. ft. (34.56 sq. m.)
TOTAL FLOOR AREA: 913 sq. ft. (84.78 sq. m.)

ABOVE AND BELOW: Wood floors, glass walls, and a repeated lightweight steel truss give this house its character. The living/dining room is loftlike and intended to be a flexible party space. The kitchen is simply arrayed along one wall, but room is found for a professional range.

The topmost floor is a triangular "spare room," which can be used for guests, work, or as a child's room.

The bedroom floor is cozy, yet open, with drawers fitted into the bed and large closets along the rear wall.

The exterior is striking and undomestic, and the house fits the site with barely inches to spare. A long skylight runs the length of the roof.

The entry is set behind the covered parking space on the ground floor. In addition to the staircase up to the living room, this floor houses a studio space, a large storage room, and a toilet.

The bathroom is compact and open, with a footed tub for fun and large glass windows for light. (See also detail on page 108.)

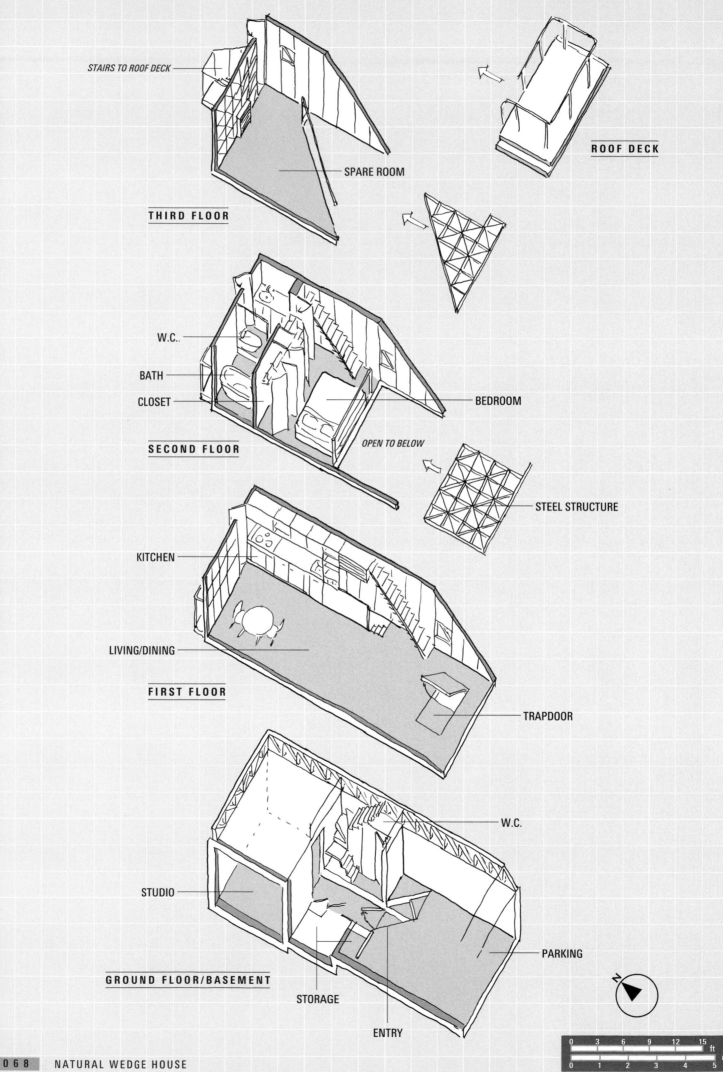

STAIRS TO ROOF DECK

ROOF DECK

SPARE ROOM

THIRD FLOOR

W.C..

BATH

CLOSET

BEDROOM

SECOND FLOOR

OPEN TO BELOW

STEEL STRUCTURE

KITCHEN

LIVING/DINING

FIRST FLOOR

TRAPDOOR

W.C.

STUDIO

PARKING

GROUND FLOOR/BASEMENT

STORAGE

ENTRY

0 3 6 9 12 15 ft
0 1 2 3 4 5 m

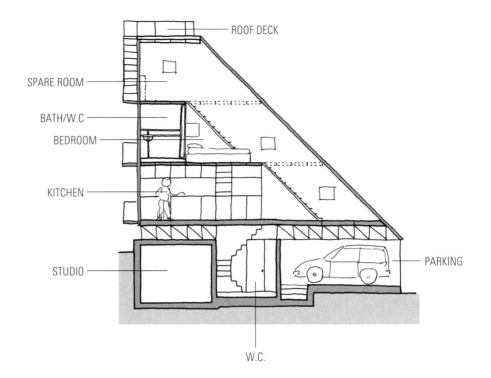

ROOF DECK

SPARE ROOM

BATH/W.C

BEDROOM

KITCHEN

STUDIO

PARKING

W.C.

When developing the concept for this radical house, architect Masaki Endoh was concerned first and foremost with light. This narrow site (about 15 feet/4.5 meters in width) faces north, and is hemmed in at the front and rear; further, the open plot to the left would probably be built to several stories in the not too distant future. The striking 45-degree triangular shape both complies with code restrictions concerning height and allows as much light as possible to enter through a long narrow skylight running up the sloping roof. The well-engineered main structure, which is based on a 2-by-2-foot (60-by-60-cm.) steel grid, diagonally reinforced throughout, is propped up above the concrete foundation walls of the ground floor, made necessary by the steep slope of the site itself. This ground floor houses parking, storage, a 116-square-foot (10.8-sq.-m.) music studio space, a small lavatory, and the entrance to the house itself. The gap between the concrete walls and the house proper is one of several features intended to optimize the ventilation through the house.

One of the more striking aspects of the home is the treatment of the exterior walls. Desiring a well-insulated wall that would nevertheless bring in as much light as possible, Endoh developed an innovative sandwich of translucent polyester fiberfill, translucent Gore-tex (for ultraviolet protection), and glass. The result is a space suffused with light during the day, which glows like a lantern at night when interior lights are turned on. The glass provides a sophisticated wall surface with a luxurious sheen that plays an intriguing counterpoint to the industrial, high-tech steel framing. Maple flooring in the first-floor living area lends a warm contrast.

The actual layout of the house is straightforward: a single 320-square-foot (30-sq.-m.) open space on the first floor provides unpartitioned living, dining, and kitchen, and suits the party-giving lifestyle of the young owners. It also has a large trapdoor in the floor over the parking area for moving large items like beds and furniture in and out of the house. The kitchen itself is adequate for a bachelor or young couple, and utilizes a commercial-grade range and half-height refrigerator. An open-framed steel staircase leads to the second floor, which holds the unenclosed master bedroom and the bath, the two divided by a deep closet. The stairs continue upward to a loftlike spare room, whose triangular floor outline echoes the profile of the house; the space can serve as a guest room, child's room, or, as at present, a secluded relaxation space. Finally, there is exterior access to a small roof terrace. Essentially, the house is a lightfilled atrium whose floors are visually separated by the delicate white structural grid. People feel compelled to investigate it, to think about the house itself, and it seems to encourage social interaction and a lively, ad-hoc way of life.

T. R. HOUSE

A private panorama brings the outside in

DESIGN: Yoshiaki Tezuka & Hirono Koike, K. T. Architecture
CONSTRUCTION: steel frame / 3 floors
OCCUPANTS: young couple
LOT: 747 sq. ft. (69.42 sq. m.)
HOUSE: 317 sq. ft. (29.43 sq. m.)
TOTAL FLOOR AREA: 742 sq. ft. (68.94 sq. m.)

By perching the living room on the topmost floor and surrounding it with a band of high windows, a bright, open, but private space was created. The panoramic view takes in trees and rooftops.

The bedroom, on the ground floor, is slightly sunken and dark-floored. Futons are stored in the closet under the sculptural staircase when not in use.

The unusual cantilever allows for a larger living room above and parking below. It also frames an attractive view of a shrine.

The second floor houses the bath, laundry, toilet, and additional closet space. Light reflecting off of the red door suffuses the space with an attractive pinkish light. Light fixtures, the sink, and other elements were chosen for their sculptural qualities.

Maintaining the panoramic view in the living room meant keeping it free of tall obstructions. Other than the line of low kitchen cabinets, the only other visible storage is a half-height bookcase that also functions as a stair rail.

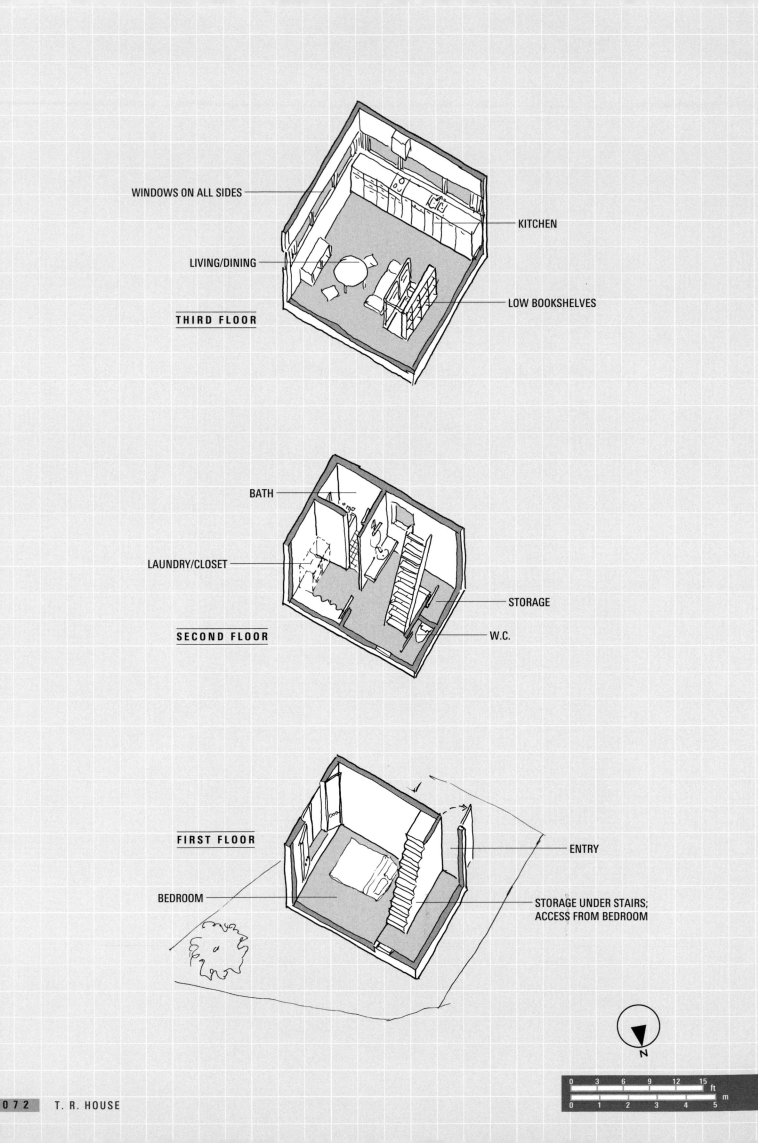

WINDOWS ON ALL SIDES

KITCHEN

LIVING/DINING

LOW BOOKSHELVES

THIRD FLOOR

BATH

LAUNDRY/CLOSET

STORAGE

SECOND FLOOR

W.C.

FIRST FLOOR

ENTRY

BEDROOM

STORAGE UNDER STAIRS;
ACCESS FROM BEDROOM

N

0 3 6 9 12 15 ft
0 1 2 3 4 5 m

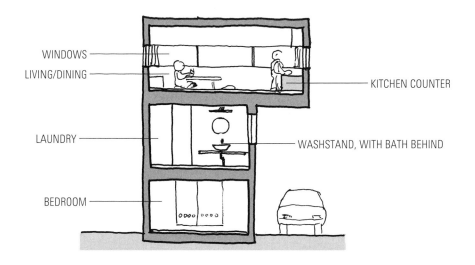

WINDOWS
LIVING/DINING
KITCHEN COUNTER
LAUNDRY
WASHSTAND, WITH BATH BEHIND
BEDROOM

Situated on a quiet street that was a rural lane only a few years ago, this 750-square-foot (70-sq.-m.) house has an intentionally top-heavy appearance. Intended to be slighty surreal, the large overhang is also a practical response to the particularities of the site; it allows for a narrow parking space and for an attractive tree-filled shrine beyond to be framed as a view as one approaches. The Big Idea was to place the living space on top, to maximize its floor area and to take advantage of the unobstructed vista by using panoramic windows. The cantilever required thoughtful engineering, but the result is that while seated in the living room one is surrounded by trees and sky; the space has a surprising sense of privacy. This room has a single long white counter that accommodates kitchen appliances, including a half-height refrigerator, as well as miscellaneous storage; a small bookcase frames one side of the stairwell.

Resolving the rest of the design necessitated one major decision: where to place the bedroom? If the bedroom went on the second floor, the bathroom would have to be on the first, and vice versa. Weighing the advantages and disadvantages of each combination, the designers and clients decided that a second-floor bathroom would be equidistant from a first-floor bedroom and the third-floor living room, and so that choice was made. One enters from the ground floor into a short concrete-floored corridor that receives light from low windows. From the outside, these windows reveal nothing more than peoples' feet. From there, one can either step down into a dark-floored bedroom, which has large perforated shutters and is partially framed by the staircase, or take the stairs to the right. Ascending into the bathroom foyer, one is enveloped in a warm pinkish light, the result of natural sunlight pouring in from the living room above and reflecting off a bright red bathroom door onto all-white walls, floors, a sculptural washbasin, and a countertop. It is an arrestingly beautiful and unexpected ambience. Walking up to the living room, which after the narrow bath area feels incredibly expansive and bright, one's attention is immediately drawn to the green treetops outside. The overall sequence of movement through the house is dynamic, surprising, and poetic.

The owner of the house works in the design field, is a fan of contemporary design, and has carefully selected a few favorite items of furniture to complement the all-white interior. A simple light fixture or appliance takes on a heightened presence here, and a small touch of color, like a bright, patterned rug, has an unexpectedly large effect. It is clear that living in this house comfortably means keeping relatively few possessions, a choice many might find difficult. But the couple is happy, and find their house to be a gratifyingly rich environment.

HOUSE IN KYODO
Separate realms for three adults

DESIGN: Hoichiro Itai & Section R Architects
CONSTRUCTION: wood / 2 floors
OCCUPANTS: couple & elderly mother
LOT: 1,077 sq. ft. (100.07 sq. m.)
HOUSE: 638 sq. ft. (59.28 sq. m.)
TOTAL FLOOR AREA: 995 sq. ft. (92.40 sq. m.)

The living/dining room on the second story of this inward-facing house has large expanses of glass that face the plant-filled deck. Ventilation has been carefully worked out with louvered windows and wooden grilles. The spiral stair leads to the husband's study below. This room is the primary gathering place for the whole family.

The exterior presents a trim facade that seems nearly impregnable. There is room to park one car alongside the gatelike entrance.

The wife's private zone on the ground floor is configured like an apartment, with a bedroom-sitting area backed by a glass-walled shared bath.

Upon entering through the main gateway, one can either ascend the exterior stairway to the mother's garden deck, turn immediately into the husband's study, or enter the wife's private zone through another door.

The study is laid out for work or small meetings, and its exposed wooden structure gives it a sense of warmth and solidity. The bookshelves are integrated into the wall structure. The spiral stair leads to the living/dining/kitchen above, while the sliding polycarbonate door opens to a bedroom nook to the left.

The husband's bedroom nook is wonderfully compact, and makes use of a short wall for housing the air conditioner, a fold down end table, lighting, and miscellaneous storage. The corridor beyond leads to a mini-kitchen and the shared bath. (See also details on pages 106 and 109.)

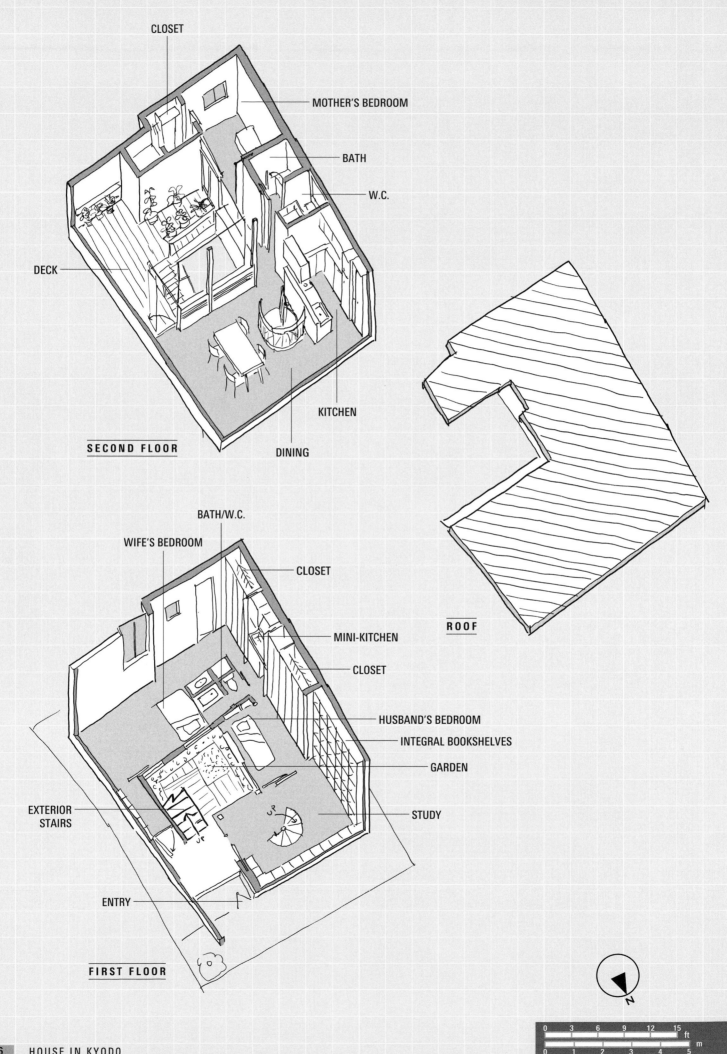

CLOSET

MOTHER'S BEDROOM

BATH

W.C.

DECK

KITCHEN

SECOND FLOOR

DINING

BATH/W.C.

WIFE'S BEDROOM

CLOSET

MINI-KITCHEN

CLOSET

HUSBAND'S BEDROOM

INTEGRAL BOOKSHELVES

GARDEN

EXTERIOR
STAIRS

STUDY

ENTRY

FIRST FLOOR

ROOF

N

0 3 6 9 12 15
ft
0 1 2 3 4 5
m

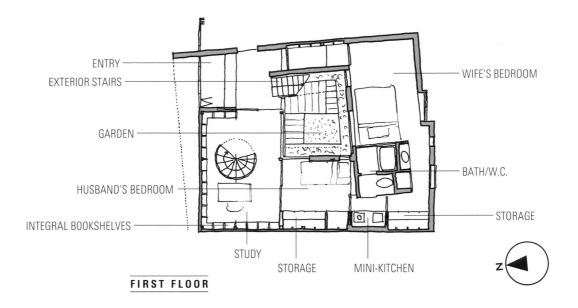

FIRST FLOOR

The House in Kyodo was designed by architect Hoichiro Itai for himself, his wife, and his elderly mother. Due to varying work and travel schedules, as well as a shared desire for a large dose of solitude with their togetherness, each of the three family members wanted to have their own "realm" within the house: spaces where they could spend time alone. Passing through the gateway gives way to a sheltered outdoor entry foyer, where one can choose to enter the husband's study to the right, the wife's zone to the left, or ascend the stairs to the mother's terrace. The result is an intricately connected but carefully articulated home that is a lot like a little courtyard village. Itai has handled the difficulties of the program in an inspired way.

Each occupant has his or her own sitting area—in the case of the architect himself, it is his book-lined study, which acts as a home office and is placed in the most visible location off of the main entry. There is a small kitchenette here as well, a comfortable bed nook (see detail on page 106), and a short corridor connecting his realm with that of his wife's. Her space boasts a small atrium, which gains more height for her rear window. It has the most convenient access to the ground-floor bath, and what amounts to a separate entryway.

The most striking feature of the house is the courtyard. The downstairs' portion is a small terrace, no bigger than a light well really, but decked with jarrah wood, bordered with large river stones, and planted with short-blade grass. An openwork steel stair with wood treads leads to the larger upper deck, which the architect's mother has turned into a garden of potted plants. Her own bedroom/sitting area opens onto this terrace, which receives the best sunlight, so she has an extremely personal and comfortable indoor-outdoor area to call her own. Inside, access to the second floor is provided by a spiral staircase leading from the ground floor study to the dining area above. The dining area is the primary communal space of the house; and there is no living room to speak of, though there is enough space for large gatherings. Completing the second floor is a kitchen and a large bath, both placed conveniently close to the mother's room.

Itai makes use of a number of space-expanding illusions, such as a gently sloping wall surrounding the upstairs terrace; generating a false sense of perspective, it gives the impression that the space is receding farther than it really is. Also, almost every vista, and particularly the one the viewer first encounters upon entering, is diagonal and upward. A look at the floor plan shows that diagonally angled walls are used extensively. Itai also skillfully balances open-feeling spaces (like the glass enclosed study, which affords an unobstructed view of the courtyard) with enclosures that seem to step back in layers—so-called overlapping planes. But most importantly, each realm of the house has been made psychologically distinct, telegraphing its presence and identity to the others, and by traveling through the house in the winding manner the architect has devised, one feels that one has traveled quite a distance and visited many different spots along the way.

HOUSE IN KAMAKURA
Intimate and dynamic cottage under the trees

DESIGN: Tomoyuki Utsumi, Milligram Studio
CONSTRUCTION: wood / 2 floors + loft
OCCUPANTS: couple
LOT: 1,779 sq. ft. (165.29 sq. m.)
HOUSE: 581 sq. ft. (53.94 sq. m.)
TOTAL FLOOR AREA: 926 sq. ft. (86.04 sq. m.)

This house is arrayed on levels, with the entry leading directly to a long triangular living room. The sunken kitchen lies beyond, and features a convenient and comfortable bar counter. A single flight of stairs leads to the bedroom and bath above. The wooded plot itself provides enough privacy to allow window shades to be kept open.

The house is carefully nestled among pryized trees, and when seen from the exterior, the way the low living room volume fits under the high, slope-roofed main volume is readily apparent.

The angular bathroom is tucked into a rear corner of the second floor, and uses a glass wall to separate the bath proper from the toilet and washbasin area while admitting natural light in through a transom window.

The second floor is also arranged on split levels, three to be exact. Arriving at the top of the stairs, one may continue on the same level to the bath, ascend a few more steps (seen here) and cross a glass-walled bridge to reach the laundry and storage area, or descend a few steps to the bedroom itself (to the right but not shown). In practice it is an easy, natural flow of circulation, one which provides an entertaining sequence of shifting vistas.

The semi-basement space under the bedroom is a private nook for the husband's musical activities. A desire to avoid cutting the roots of a large tree led to the use of a sloping foundation wall, and the ladder leads to the bedroom above. (See also detail on page 106.)

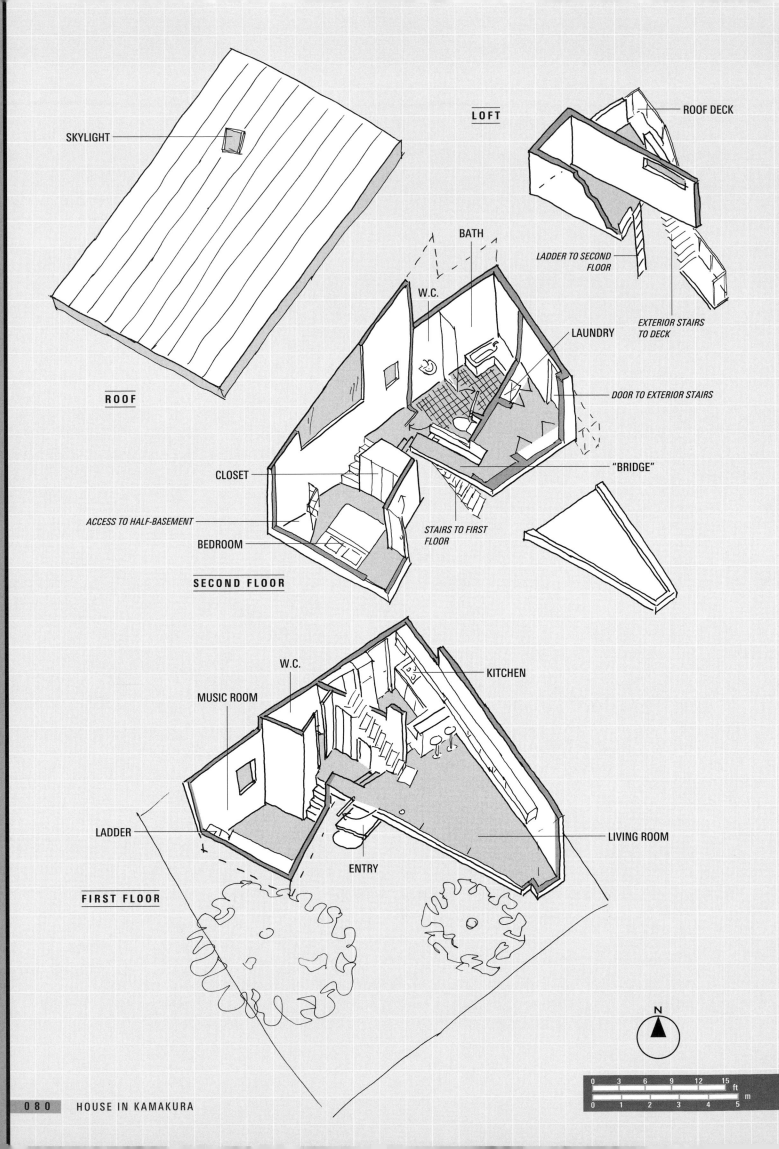

SKYLIGHT

ROOF

LOFT

ROOF DECK

LADDER TO SECOND FLOOR

EXTERIOR STAIRS TO DECK

BATH

W.C.

LAUNDRY

DOOR TO EXTERIOR STAIRS

CLOSET

"BRIDGE"

ACCESS TO HALF-BASEMENT

STAIRS TO FIRST FLOOR

BEDROOM

SECOND FLOOR

W.C.

KITCHEN

MUSIC ROOM

LADDER

LIVING ROOM

ENTRY

FIRST FLOOR

N

0 3 6 9 12 15 ft
0 1 2 3 4 5 m

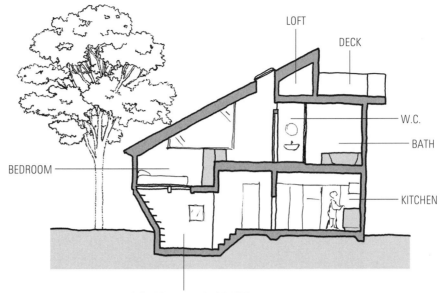

LOFT

DECK

W.C.

BATH

BEDROOM

KITCHEN

MUSIC ROOM (HALF-BASEMENT)

The site for this house in the historic city of Kamakura is a generous 1,780 square feet (165 sq. m.). Kamakura, however, is one of the few communities in Japan that has enacted laws for preserving trees within the city environs, and this site is blessed with two beautiful protected specimens whose location severely limited the designer's options. The result is a multilevel wood-frame house, angled snugly back into the far corner of the site—part of which seems to float—and displaying a prominent sloped roof. I say "multilevel" rather than "multistory" because architect Tomoyuki Utsumi of Milligram Studio has elaborated what is basically a two-story home into a highly modulated structure with no fewer than five distinct interior levels. Although the structure occupies less than half the lot size, the result is a constant impression of greater space—of continuation and an ongoing sequence of surprise.

The overall atmosphere is spare and modern, with occasional luxurious touches such as marble flooring in the entry area. Yet the home is casual and inviting—a bar counter separating the sunken kitchen from the living room is a natural magnet for lingering conversation. The house has a playful spirit: bridges and ladders, one or two short doorways perfectly scaled for children (if ever the owners decide to have them), a seemingly underground music room with a sloping wall (actually designed to minimize cutting the roots of the large cherry tree on the lot) and reached from the bedroom by one of the ladders (see detail on page 106). There is a large storage loft, which forms a kind of intimate third floor, and other storage tucked everywhere, including a place for shoes under the entryway stairs. The architect has also provided for future expansion, with a doorway already located on the second floor under the generous overhanging eaves.

The house overcomes its limited floor area by being dynamic and geometric, by keeping successive spaces partially hidden, and by making every view move upward and over an architectural element. Finally, the long, triangular ground-floor living room, the largest space in the house, is fronted by a wall of plate glass, providing an immense view of the trees and the garden outside. True, there are many occasions for closing the full-length blinds, but because of the view, this house manages to be snug and sheltering, yet open wide to the surroundings.

HOUSE IN KAGURAZAKA
Convertible space for gatherings

DESIGN: Mikan
CONSTRUCTION: steel frame / 3 floors
OCCUPANTS: family of four
LOT: 884 sq. ft. (82.14 sq. m.)
HOUSE: 529 sq. ft. (49.10 sq. m.)
TOTAL FLOOR AREA: 1,126 sq. ft. (104.61 sq. m.)

ABOVE AND BELOW: The ground floor of this house is conceived as a flexible, glass-enclosed space that serves as a family library, a large play area, and a place for gatherings such as poetry readings.

The exterior presents a utilitarian personality, and when seen from the narrow street on which it is located, the small third story is not readily apparent.

Life in the house revolves around the kitchen table, which is open to the other spaces and forms the natural center of circulation.

The main stairway leads directly to the kitchen, and can be closed by means of a fold-down panel during drafty winter months.

A large plate glass window brings light in from the third-floor bathroom area and down through the stairwell.

Much of the third floor is devoted to a large roof deck, complete with a grass lawn.

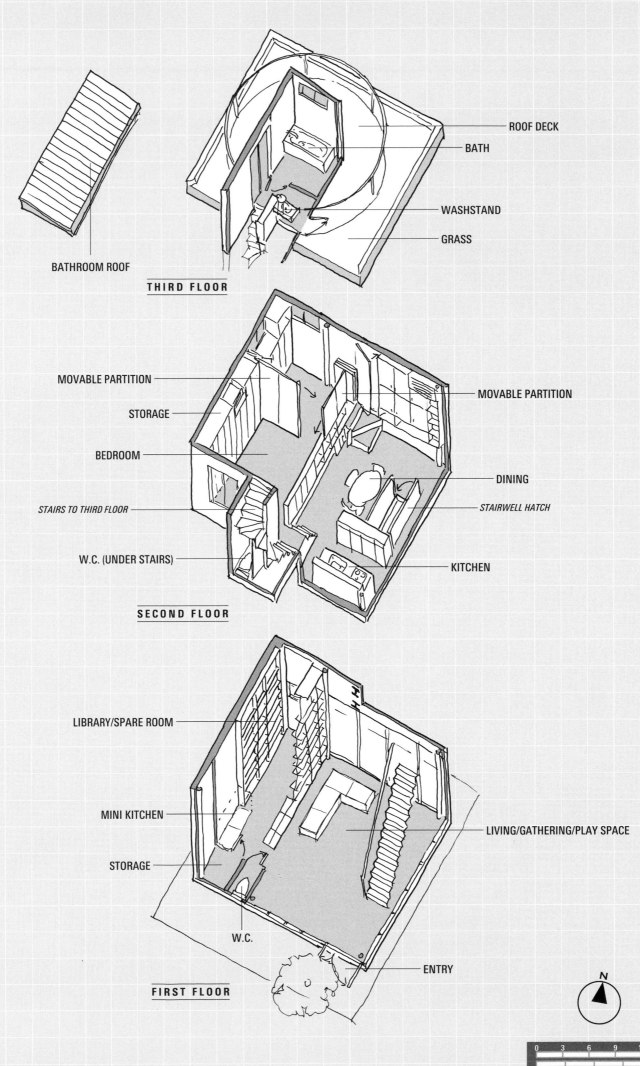

BATHROOM ROOF

THIRD FLOOR

ROOF DECK

BATH

WASHSTAND

GRASS

MOVABLE PARTITION

STORAGE

BEDROOM

STAIRS TO THIRD FLOOR

W.C. (UNDER STAIRS)

SECOND FLOOR

MOVABLE PARTITION

DINING

STAIRWELL HATCH

KITCHEN

LIBRARY/SPARE ROOM

MINI KITCHEN

STORAGE

W.C.

FIRST FLOOR

LIVING/GATHERING/PLAY SPACE

ENTRY

N

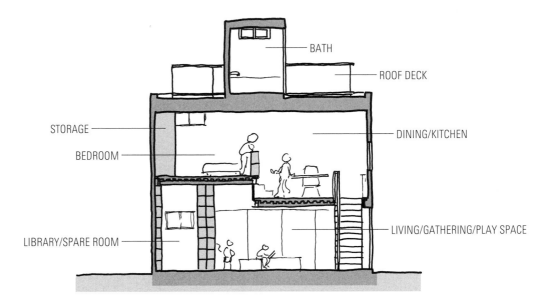

STORAGE —

BEDROOM —

LIBRARY/SPARE ROOM —

BATH

ROOF DECK

DINING/KITCHEN

LIVING/GATHERING/PLAY SPACE

The Kagurazaka neighborhood is one of the oldest in Tokyo, and even in the Edo period (1600–1868) it was densely populated. A hallmark of Japanese neighborhoods of the pre-vehicular age was the siting of row-houses and tenements along narrow alleys, and many such alleys remain in use today. This steel-frame house by architectural firm Mikan has no vehicular access, and is very close to its neighbors, but the lane it fronts is refreshingly quiet. If the owners, who can reach anywhere they need on foot or by train, ever decide they need a car, they will be able to rent a parking space nearby, a common practice in Japanese urban areas. So the fact that no parking was needed was a blessing. But the narrow alley forced the architects to consider both the actual height and the apparent scale of the house; and though it appears from nearly all vantage points to be only two stories, it is actually three, the uppermost being small and set back.

An unusual feature of this house is the absence of a living room in the conventional sense. Instead, the owners asked for an open ground floor to be used as a library/study space and for occasional poetry read-ings and other gatherings. Walled with large expanses of glass, this room has shelves for over 8,000 books, and is a true multipurpose area: for play, work, or entertaining. The second floor, meanwhile, is split into two levels, the lower devoted to the kitchen and dining area and surrounded by storage, the upper being the bedrooms, with a wall of closets. These two levels basically form one space, but the designers have devised a nice system of folding panels to close off the bedroom when desired (see detail on page 98). Surprisingly, the clients did not ask for a separate bedroom for the children, deciding that a simple folding partition would suffice, but the house will be easy to modify for more privacy in the future. A light-filled stairway that can-tilevers out from the rest of the house and gives it a jauntier profile leads to the third floor, which has a small bathroom and a large outdoor terrace that enjoys fine views of the city.

Despite the use of industrial materials and its exposed steel structure, the house has a very homey feel, largely due to the way in which the dining table has been allowed to become the center of family life. The main flow of circulation converges here, and those seated at the table can even see downstairs. Further, the placement and size of the storage in this room puts everything within easy reach, and the low cabinets run-ning between the bedrooms and the table allow everyone to feel the broad expanse of the upper level while the beds remain hidden from view. All in all, this is a sensitive design, eminently flexible and practical.

ENGAWA HOUSE

Wide-open family room with a wall of storage

DESIGN: Takaharu Tezuka & Yui Tezuka, Tezuka Architects; Masahiro Ikeda, Mias

CONSTRUCTION: wood & steel frame / 1 floor

OCCUPANTS: family of four

LOT: 2,113 sq. ft. (196.27 sq. m.)

HOUSE: 845 sq. ft. (78.48 sq. m.)

TOTAL FLOOR AREA: 845 sq. ft. (78.48 sq. m.)

An unusual approach to building a family compound, this house shares the parents' garden, and was sited and scaled so as to avoid casting the parents' home in shadow. An *engawa* is a porchlike outdoor corridor which acts like an extension of the rooms within, and this house reinterprets this traditional verandalike feature.

From the street side, the house appears to be a solid, wood-sided box with a band of high windows. The entry is on the right-hand side.

The interior is composed of a single large, high-ceilinged room which is filled with natural light from two sides.
The kitchen is arranged on a stainless steel island, paired with an enormous table, the center of family life.
A movable wall of shelving separates the children's area from the living area. The child is sitting on a catwalk
formed by a line of cabinets that run the length of the house.

The parents' bedroom is sunny and simply appointed.

The children's room is flexibly laid out; all rooms
open to the veranda.

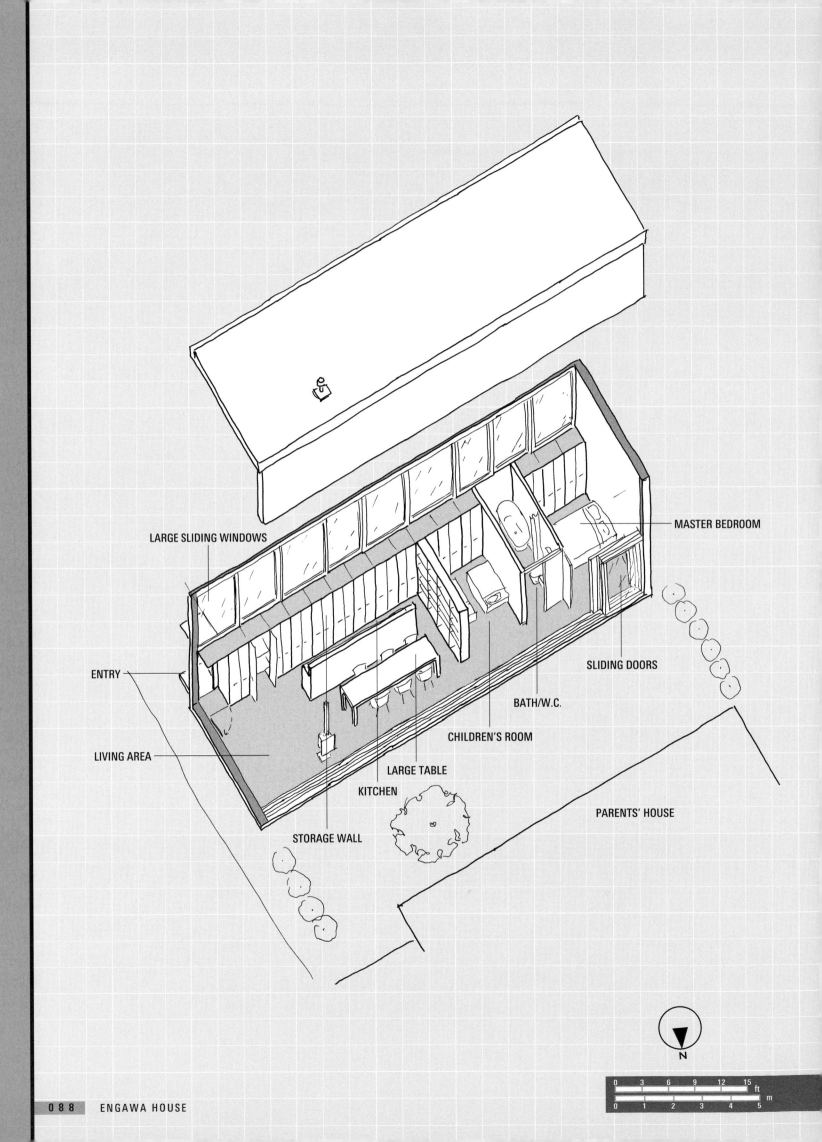

LARGE SLIDING WINDOWS

MASTER BEDROOM

ENTRY

SLIDING DOORS

BATH/W.C.

LIVING AREA

CHILDREN'S ROOM

LARGE TABLE

KITCHEN

PARENTS' HOUSE

STORAGE WALL

N

0   3   6   9   12   15
ft

0   1   2   3   4   5
m

It is difficult to envision a house simpler than this. Basically a long, low box 14 3/4 feet wide and 11 1/2 feet high (4.5 m. by 3.5 m.), the interior is a single, loosely divided space that uses no full-height partitions. Full advantage is taken of the high ceiling by leaving the entire upper third of the interior unobstructed. Even the bathroom is open at the top. The idea for the house, by the husband-and-wife team of Tezuka and Tezuka, was suggested by the site and the close proximity of the owners' parents.

The proposed house was to bound the parents' garden, replacing a wall that blocked the light to their home. The problem was to build in a way that maximized the light while allowing both houses to share the remaining garden space. The available sunlight suggested a maximum height of 11 1/2 feet (3.5 m.) and a distance from the existing house of about 13 feet (4 m.); in this way the exterior dimensions were set.

The window arrangement was also a response to sunlight as well as a desire for privacy, since the house needed to be placed very close to the street. The architects judged that placing the street-side openings above a 6 1/2-foot height (2 m.) would provide the desired privacy and allow for ample storage along that wall. Fifteen 3-foot-wide (90-cm.), 2-foot-deep (60-cm.), double-doored cabinets were built to form an immense 565-cubic-foot (16-cu.-m.) storage wall, and they were made strong enough to be used as a catwalk, allowing access to the curtains and windows overhead. The garden-side wall is the reverse, with the upper part closed and the lower 6 1/2 feet (2 m.) made of a series of wide, wooden sliding glass doors, nine in all, that allow the house to be entirely opened on the side facing the parents' home. These long, unobstructed openings are simple in concept, but necessitated a bit of engineering and the use of long steel beams; in fact, the house can be considered a hybrid wood/steel structure, with a steel-box frame married to a wood frame.

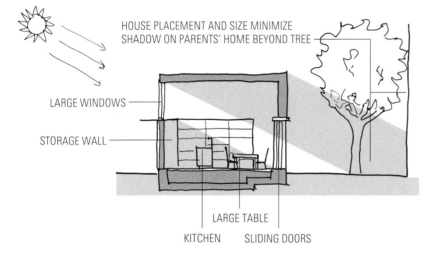

HOUSE PLACEMENT AND SIZE MINIMIZE
SHADOW ON PARENTS' HOME BEYOND TREE

LARGE WINDOWS

STORAGE WALL

LARGE TABLE

KITCHEN   SLIDING DOORS

The division of space is straightforward. The bathroom needed solid walls, and some sort of door was desired for the master bedroom; the plumbing connections for the kitchen would be stationary. But other than that, the owners assume that the interior arrangement will change over time. In particular, the children's room will evolve as the children grow and their needs change; at the moment, their room is divided from the living/dining area by a movable bookshelf, and has no door.

The kitchen is essentially a 14 3/4-foot-long (4.5-m.) half-height stainless steel divider, housing a commercial grade sink, stove, half-height (but capacious) refrigerator, and countertops, and is quite ample for preparing meals that include a number of guests as well. This divider is paired with a custom-built dining table 11 1/2 feet long (3.5 m.) made of laminated Finnish plywood and whose proportion and shape echo that of the house itself. A table like this becomes the center of family life: the preferred location for work as well as conversation, a place for resting as well as eating.

Other amenities include underfloor heating to offset drafts in the cold months, and a small wood-burning stove, a trademark of the Tezukas' residential designs. Poetic as well as practical, it stands near the table like a beloved household retainer. The flooring and door frames are pine, the cabinetry has a birch veneer, and the exterior siding is teak, which will age beautifully. The designers have generated a warm, sensitive, even traditional-feeling family environment through the use of such a radically simple and modern overall form, and the manner in which it forms a multigenerational home compound with the parents' house is actually a return to an older idea that is still very attractive to many people.

KU ENUMA HOUSE
Handmade uniqueness on an "impossible" site

DESIGN: Takekazu Murayama
CONSTRUCTION: wood & reinforced concrete / 2 floors
OCCUPANTS: couple with large dog
LOT: 1,203 sq. ft. (111.72 sq. m.)
HOUSE: 664 sq. ft. (61.71 sq. m.)
TOTAL FLOOR AREA: 1,123 sq. ft. (104.29 sq. m.) + 115 sq. ft. (10.73 sq. m.) for loft

Reminiscent of traditional Japanese farmhouses, the interior of this long, narrow house is open, warm, and inviting. The bedroom shown here is arranged on two levels, joined by wide stairs that serve as seating.

RIGHT, FAR RIGHT: The entrance lies roughly in the middle of the house, and is a spacious atrium with wooden staircases and a ramp that lead directly to the main living areas on the various levels. Like the garden, this atrium functions as an important light well.

The narrow lot for this home was originally a long driveway, which gives the finished structure its seemingly impossible narrowness and length.

With exposed beams and a traditional wooden tub, the bathhouse is a luxurious but rustic space that immerses the occupants in tradition.

◀ The snug kitchen opens onto a small garden, which brings natural light into the house at this end. A separate bathhouse lies beyond.

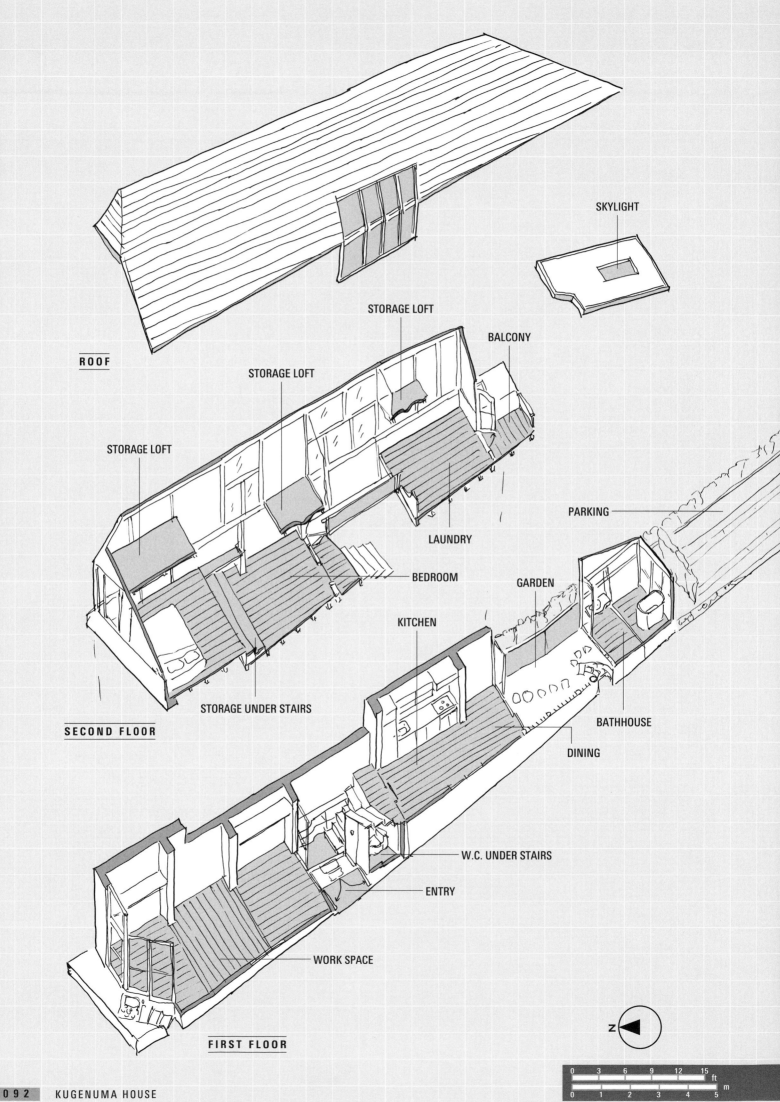

ROOF

SKYLIGHT

STORAGE LOFT

STORAGE LOFT

BALCONY

STORAGE LOFT

PARKING

LAUNDRY

BEDROOM

GARDEN

KITCHEN

STORAGE UNDER STAIRS

BATHHOUSE

SECOND FLOOR

DINING

W.C. UNDER STAIRS

ENTRY

WORK SPACE

FIRST FLOOR

N

0 3 6 9 12 15 ft
0 1 2 3 4 5 m

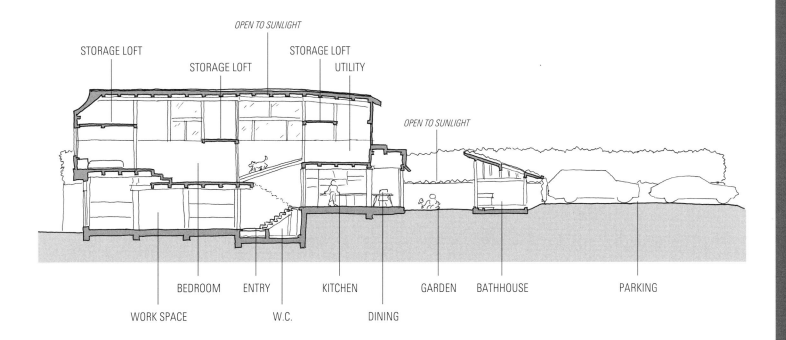

OPEN TO SUNLIGHT

STORAGE LOFT
STORAGE LOFT
STORAGE LOFT
UTILITY

OPEN TO SUNLIGHT

WORK SPACE
BEDROOM ENTRY KITCHEN GARDEN BATHHOUSE PARKING
W.C. DINING

The unlikeliest of houses, this handsome and lovingly detailed 1,120-square-foot (104-sq.-m.) house was built in a long driveway. As is often the case in Japan, family property was divided among siblings and thanks to an inspired design by architect Takekazu Murayama, what was once the long narrow entry route into the main lot became the site of a surprisingly comfortable and spacious home. Indeed the site is nearly impossible to build on: not only is it narrow—13 feet (4 m.) at the widest, narrowing to 7 feet (2.2 m.) at one point—but the long eastern side runs along a 10-foot-high (3-m.) concrete retaining wall, supporting the ground on which the neighbors' house is built. Faced with dual structural and spatial problems, Murayama's entirely code-conforming solution was to seek the neighbors' permission to buttress their retaining wall with another that would form a solid two-story main structure for the new house on the eastern side, and to divide the house itself into five linear segments, in which enclosed spaces alternate with open or skylit ones. He utilized a variety of level changes to modulate the interior scale and to enhance the flow of circulation, all while remembering that a large dog was an important family member.

The entryway itself, near the center of the house, is a stunningly lit two-story atrium. Immediately to the left is a 290-square-foot (27-sq.-m.) work space from which the couple runs their electronic component business. Climbing up a few stairs to the right, one enters the kitchen/dining area, a small garden visible through wooden sliding doors, and beyond that, the detached bathhouse. More than just an offbeat feature, the bathhouse is one key to making the entire design workable. Separating it from the rest of the house allows ample natural light into the dining/kitchen and utility areas, and although the resulting gap could have been treated as a glass-roofed light well, an actual open-air garden is much more attractive and paradoxically increases the sense of privacy.

The second floor above the work space is occupied by the capacious two-level bedroom. So much beautifully joined and detailed exposed wood is used that one fails to notice the clearly visible concrete wall that supports the house. Tremendous carpentry skill is displayed in the roof structure, which tapers and slopes in a boatlike fashion. There is grass growing on the bathhouse roof, and a tiny terrace off the laundry room provides an intimate perch over the garden. Every door is unique and handmade, and a wooden bathtub lends even more of a rustic Japanese flair. The house is lavished with practical details as well, such as the large volume of storage under the wide bedroom stairs, which double as seating. The overall impression: a warm, inviting, comfortable residence that is fun to move around in, and that seems to blend equal parts Japanese farmhouse and Northern California hippie haven.

PART II

DETAILS THAT MAKE A DIFFERENCE

While intelligent and enlightened overall planning is the most essential feature of a well-designed small house, often it is the details that make it truly livable and add character. Once the basic organization of the house is decided, then it's time to pay attention to the specifics. How big are window openings? What kind of lighting should be used? The placement of passageways may have been set, but is there an opportunity to use the space to fulfill another function? Answering questions like "How big?", "How wide?", "Does it move?", and "Can I shut it away?" are the essence of architectural detailing for convenience and ease. When well considered, details can make the difference between having a house that is barely adequate and one that is interesting and even fun to live in.

Every designer has his or her own approach to detailing of course, and each client has strong notions of beauty and convenience. Some architects, for instance, revel in details, and are happy to sketch cabinets, drawer pulls, window frames, and movable partitions for hours on end; others feel they can do no more than select a few unusual items from a manufacturer's catalog. Or a homeowner may honestly prefer an "unde-tailed" look. But the kind of inventiveness that emerges when common problems are solved with élan can make a house much more enjoyable to live in. In the best cases, they can reflect the occupants' personalities and even enhance their better characteristics.

This is not to imply that details are always afterthoughts. In fact, to work well they must often be part of a Big Idea and brought into play early in the design process. Further, very few aspects of home design can be thought about in isolation from other factors, details included. It is the synergy of complementary or even opposing elements that really generates a spark of life in a living space, the ways in which taking care of one need might simultaneously satisfy another.

Take the seemingly distinct requirements for a kitchen, some natural light, some storage, and a stairway. Many fine houses might be created by approaching each of these functions separately, but imagine the pos-sibility of combining them all in one unifying feature, and thereby solving most of one's space problem? The kitchen of the White Box House does just that: the kitchen, which is part of a larger integrated storage zone and is situated above a stairwell, allows light from a large skylight into the rest of the house, going as far as having a glass floor for enhancing the flow of light to the floor below. Other examples include making corri-dors primary storage areas, letting storage provide illumination, or giving a section of wall multiple duties as home to a nightstand, lighting fixture, cabinet, and decorative elements.

The following pages delve a bit more deeply into some of the more interesting details of the houses pre-sented in the previous section. Some details might be easily reproduced in another home, while others can be adapted depending upon specific conditions. A few are quite unique and are included less for their imme-diate applicability elsewhere than as examples of creative thinking and sophisticated design. They have been grouped into a handful of primary categories: Kitchens, Partitions, Storage, Light, Nooks, and Bathrooms. But as suggested above, the most interesting and generally most successful details are not easily categorized, since they solve several problems at once.

KITCHENS
When closeness is a virtue

There is no single kitchen layout that will meet the needs of everyone. People eat differently, cook differently, and have widely differing ideas about how to organize their kitchen items. Some need more space than others, and while a few want everything shut away out of sight, most of us want to have frequently used items close at hand. Regardless, lack of space makes kitchen layout all the more challenging. It may be impossible to have a fully separate kitchen; that food preparation, living, and dining will be combined in one space may seem to be a given when dealing with very small homes. Yet there is more room for choice than may be immediately apparent. As long as kitchen-related storage is adequate, one may well be able to get by with less actual counter space. What must absolutely be thought about carefully, though, is the height of things, and the amount of space one has to move around while cooking. The following details show several approaches, from an ultra-minimal kitchen for a couple whose food preparation needs are extremely simple, to a snug but surprisingly full-featured kitchen for one.

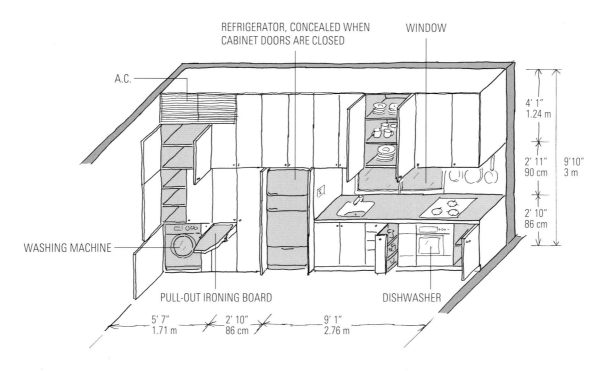

STORAGE FOR EVERY CONCEIVABLE USE; HIGH CEILING PROVIDES ADDITIONAL STORAGE SPACE, SO EVERYTHING CAN BE SHUT OUT OF SIGHT

House in Umegaoka, *page 38*: Since this house has only a single room for all living and dining functions, including cooking and laundry, meeting all the requirements without cluttering the space presented a major challenge. This wall of cabinets, with specific spaces for everything from the washing machine and ironing board to the refrigerator and rice, keeps all items close at hand but out of sight, and keeps the floor space open for seating and movement.

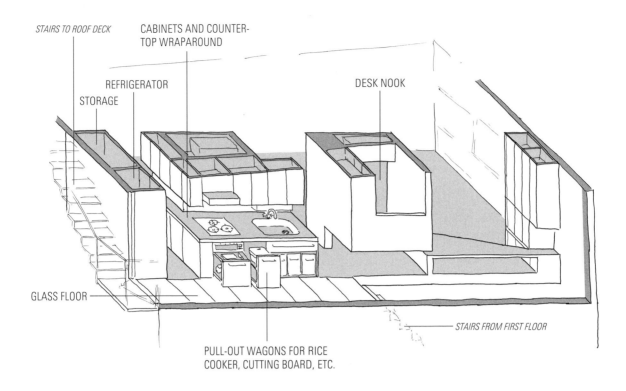

STAIRS TO ROOF DECK   CABINETS AND COUNTER-
TOP WRAPAROUND

REFRIGERATOR

STORAGE

DESK NOOK

GLASS FLOOR

STAIRS FROM FIRST FLOOR

PULL-OUT WAGONS FOR RICE
COOKER, CUTTING BOARD, ETC.

White Box House, *page 58*: This kitchen occupies a narrow area directly underneath a large skylight, the primary source of light into the house, and its glass floor allows light through to the story below. Between the kitchen and the living room is a long strip of built-in cabinets and cubicles, and the kitchen is really a part of this. The countertop is particularly well thought out, wrapping around into the passageway to the dining area, with cabinets above and below. (See also pages 101, 103, and 105.)

Nakagawa House, *page 26*: One reason this house works so well is this compact, well-designed kitchen island. The side that faces the living room is an attractive planter with handmade glass; the other side is an incredibly compact but easy-to-use cooking area. The bulk of the kitchen storage is made up of deep pull-out cabinets (indicated by dotted line). Movement in and around the cooking area is incredibly smooth and easy.

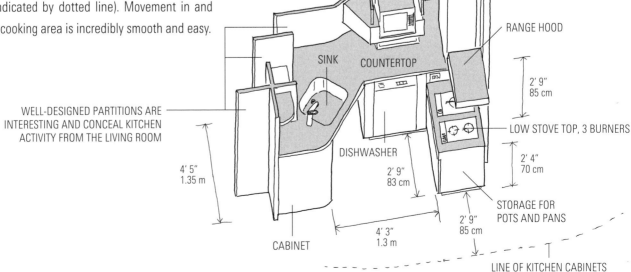

EXISTING STRUCTURAL COLUMNS

MICROWAVE OVEN,
TOASTER BELOW

HANDMADE GLASS
PARTITION/PLANTER

RANGE HOOD

SINK   COUNTERTOP

WELL-DESIGNED PARTITIONS ARE
INTERESTING AND CONCEAL KITCHEN
ACTIVITY FROM THE LIVING ROOM

2' 9"
85 cm

LOW STOVE TOP, 3 BURNERS

DISHWASHER

2' 4"
70 cm

4' 5"
1.35 m

2' 9"
83 cm

STORAGE FOR
POTS AND PANS

2' 9"
85 cm

CABINET

4' 3"
1.3 m

LINE OF KITCHEN CABINETS

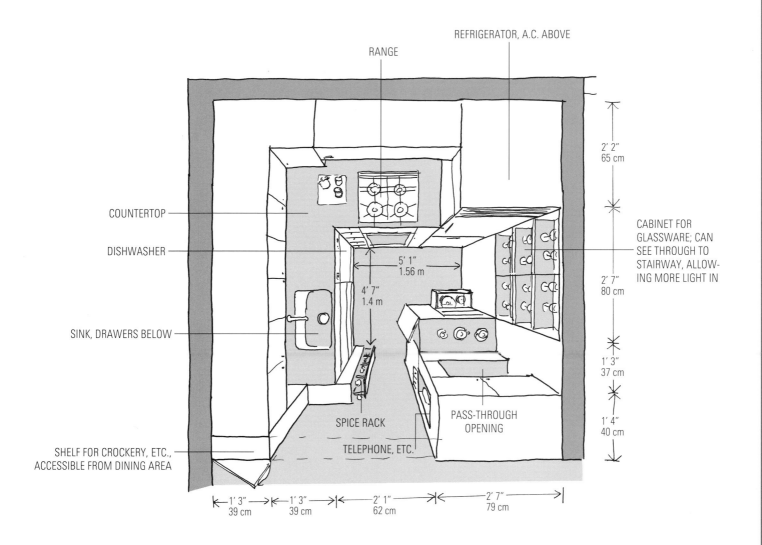

RANGE

REFRIGERATOR, A.C. ABOVE

COUNTERTOP

DISHWASHER

SINK, DRAWERS BELOW

SHELF FOR CROCKERY, ETC.,
ACCESSIBLE FROM DINING AREA

SPICE RACK

TELEPHONE, ETC.

PASS-THROUGH
OPENING

CABINET FOR
GLASSWARE; CAN
SEE THROUGH TO
STAIRWAY, ALLOW-
ING MORE LIGHT IN

2' 2"
65 cm

2' 7"
80 cm

1' 3"
37 cm

1' 4"
40 cm

5' 1"
1.56 m

4' 7"
1.4 m

1' 3"
39 cm

1' 3"
39 cm

2' 1"
62 cm

2' 7"
79 cm

Saginomiya House, *page 22*: This kitchen is for a woman who lives alone but entertains frequently. With a full kitchen downstairs for party use, this kitchen is essentially for cooking for one or two. Fit into a 7 by 7-foot-square space (2.2-sq.-m.), it is nevertheless fully equipped.

PARTITIONS

Conversion when you want it

One useful approach to making a small space seem larger is to avoid subdividing it except when absolutely necessary. Flexible partitioning strategies have a lot to contribute in many cases. Partitions need not be full height, either; configuring a wall to be partly fixed, perhaps as a mid-height storage unit, and partly filled when desired by movable elements, is one useful idea. Partitions can be used for their geometric character, color, texture, and light modulation as well.

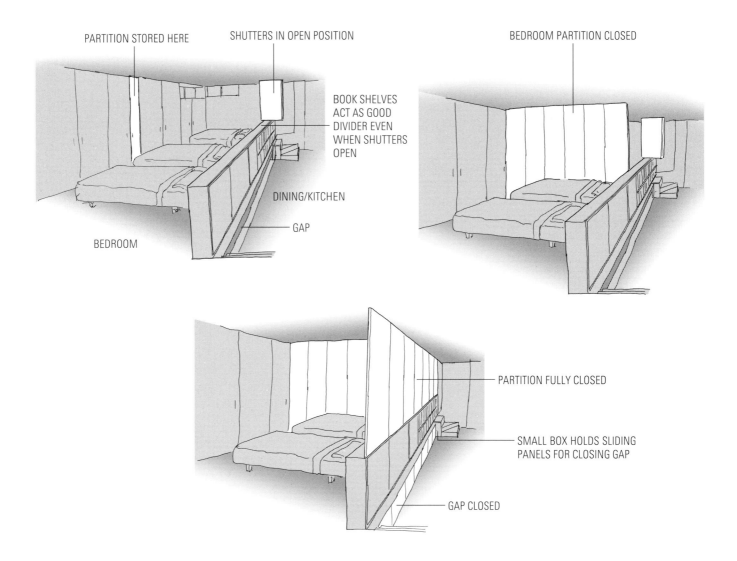

PARTITION STORED HERE

SHUTTERS IN OPEN POSITION

BEDROOM PARTITION CLOSED

BOOK SHELVES ACT AS GOOD DIVIDER EVEN WHEN SHUTTERS OPEN

DINING/KITCHEN

GAP

BEDROOM

PARTITION FULLY CLOSED

SMALL BOX HOLDS SLIDING PANELS FOR CLOSING GAP

GAP CLOSED

House in Kagurazaka, *page 82*: The main family space of this house is on the second floor, the lower kitchen and dining space to the right divided from a raised bedroom area by a half-height wall of cabinets. Beneath the cabinets is a gap which opens to the ground floor for ventilation. The designers have devised an excellent system of partitions that fills the gap above the cabinets to separate the sleeping quarters from the kitchen/dining space, and a full-height partition to divide the sleeping area into two separate rooms. A set of small shutters closes the gap beneath the shelves that opens to the floor below for ventilation, when desired.

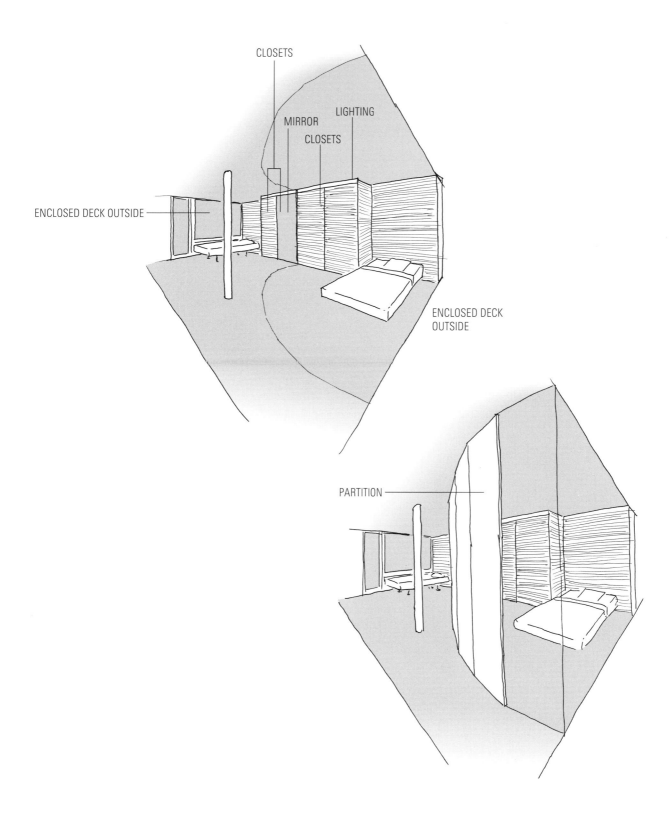

CLOSETS

MIRROR

LIGHTING

CLOSETS

ENCLOSED DECK OUTSIDE

ENCLOSED DECK OUTSIDE

PARTITION

House in Moto-Azabu, *page 30*: A familiar problem: the couple wants to be together, but one snores. How to devise separate bedrooms without seeming to cut the couple off from each other? Movable panels that sweep across the second-floor space in a broad arc provide isolation when desired but leave the space open otherwise.

STORAGE

There's always room for more

Every house needs places to put things: clothes, books, appliances, linen, entertainment, and the ever-expanding category of "miscellaneous items." Usually that means cabinets for storage, but exactly how big should they be and where should they be placed? Most of the houses featured in this book take a very straightforward and inexpensive approach to storage, with simple closets and shelves. But several show great ingenuity by utilizing commonly overlooked spaces, such as under the floor or stairs, or by using the requirement for storage elements as an opportunity to make something beautiful.

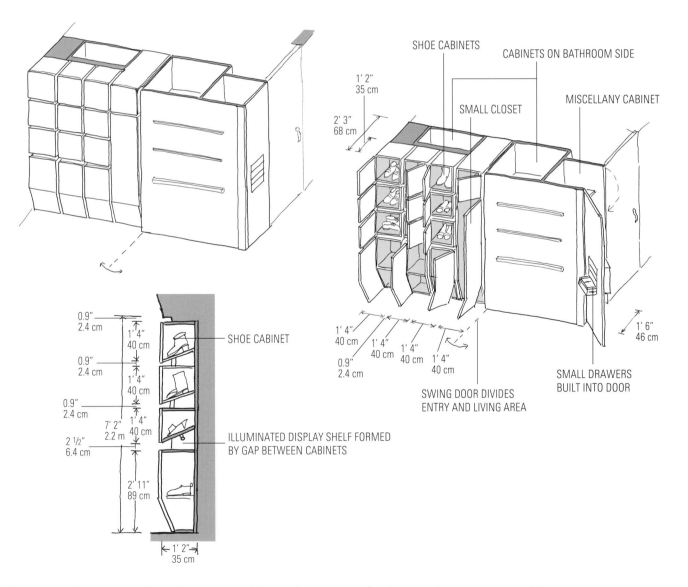

Nakagawa House, *page 26*: A shoe storage cabinet in the entryway of a Japanese house is an essential feature. In this house, the designer was able to turn this necessity into a sculptural detail, with well-articulated individual cabinets and recessed lighting. The entire wall of which it is a part divides the living area from the bath, and is devoted to storage on both sides.

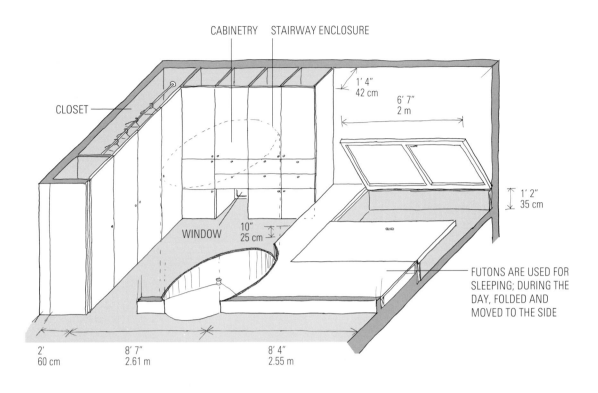

CABINETRY   STAIRWAY ENCLOSURE

CLOSET

1' 4"
42 cm

6' 7"
2 m

1' 2"
35 cm

WINDOW

10"
25 cm

FUTONS ARE USED FOR
SLEEPING; DURING THE
DAY, FOLDED AND
MOVED TO THE SIDE

2'
60 cm

8' 7"
2.61 m

8' 4"
2.55 m

House in Umegaoka, *page 38*: The architect here turned the placement of the circular steel stair shaft into an opportunity to divide the master bedroom into a storage and dressing area and a raised sleeping platform. The walls of the storage area are lined with wooden cabinets, and a small window peeks out at floor height. The sleeping platform, intended for use with futons, has storage space beneath as well.

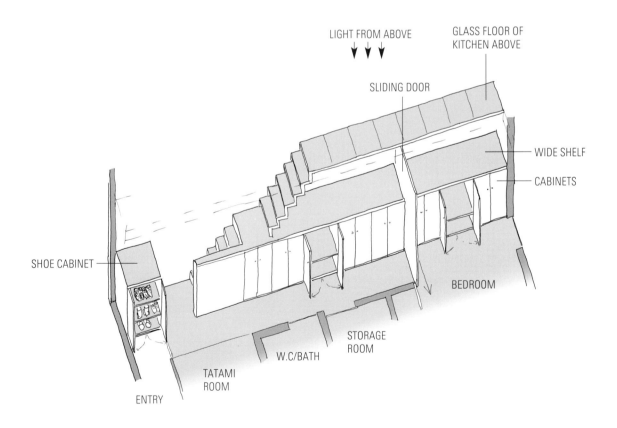

LIGHT FROM ABOVE

GLASS FLOOR OF
KITCHEN ABOVE

SLIDING DOOR

WIDE SHELF

CABINETS

SHOE CABINET

BEDROOM

STORAGE
ROOM

W.C/BATH

TATAMI
ROOM

ENTRY

White Box House, *page 58*: Because of the light spilling in from above, this area becomes simultaneously a storage area, staircase, and light well. Half-height cabinets are ample while allowing more light in than full-height ones would, and provide a wide shelf for oversized objects and display. (See also page 103.)

LIGHT

Strategies for brightening your inner world

Though some of us are forced to live or work in places with little natural light, who actually prefers to? Small houses often have the added disadvantage of being situated on narrow lots, possibly even shaded on all sides by neighboring buildings. The first thing a good designer will look at in such cases is the direction and angle of the sunlight, and then he or she will probably attempt to arrange the roof of the house and the interior spaces in order to get as much natural light inside as possible. But natural light needs to be modulated as well; sunny is good, but it is far preferable to be able to control sunlight for mood and comfort. Artificial illumination presents ample opportunity for experimentation and invention as well. Well deployed, it can seem to widen rooms, raise ceilings, or simply add mystery by suggesting there is more than meets the eye.

T-set House, *page 50*: A difficult lot allowed the architect Manabu Chiba to build a bit higher than usual, but placed restrictions on the amount of natural light that would reach the first-floor spaces. By designing a large window facing a gap between the second-floor bedroom floor and the wall, Chiba created, in effect, a diminutive atrium. The single window can illuminate both floors and the living room gains a little extra perceived height.

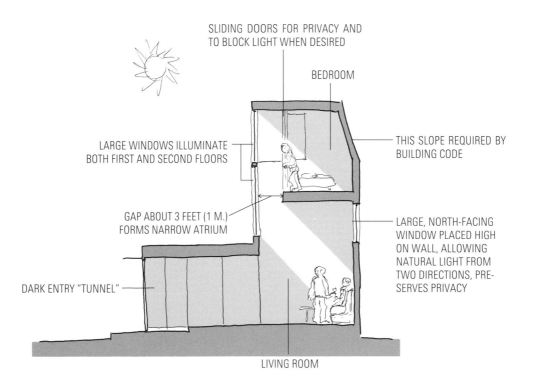

SLIDING DOORS FOR PRIVACY AND
TO BLOCK LIGHT WHEN DESIRED

BEDROOM

LARGE WINDOWS ILLUMINATE
BOTH FIRST AND SECOND FLOORS

THIS SLOPE REQUIRED BY
BUILDING CODE

GAP ABOUT 3 FEET (1 M.)
FORMS NARROW ATRIUM

LARGE, NORTH-FACING
WINDOW PLACED HIGH
ON WALL, ALLOWING
NATURAL LIGHT FROM
TWO DIRECTIONS, PRE-
SERVES PRIVACY

DARK ENTRY "TUNNEL"

LIVING ROOM

White Box House, *page 58*: This sectional view shows the glass floor-cum-skylight that allows light to filter down through the kitchen to the floor below. The light spills into the living area as well through variously shaped openings in the built-in cabinets and the desk nook.

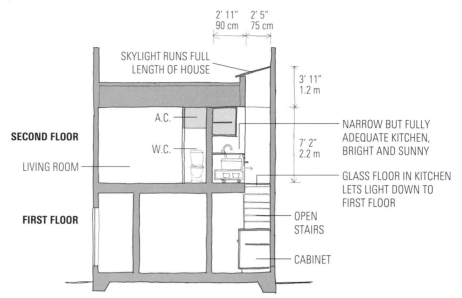

Sora no Katachi House *page 54,* While the plot and the overall layout did not allow the designer to make very wide rooms, height was used to great advantage in the dual-level living room. Desiring large, full-height windows on both the street and garden sides of the space, and wanting to be able to control not only the amount of light but also the degree of privacy, he devised a layered system derived from traditional Japanese practice. Innermost is a set of paper *shoji* screens; by allowing them to slide upward no additional floor space is required for opening them. Conventional sliding glass doors provide closure to the elements, and screen doors protect against insects. Finally, slatted wooden storm shutters are hung on tracks against the exterior wall. Regardless of whether the large windows and shutters are open or closed, light spills onto one wall from a long skylight.

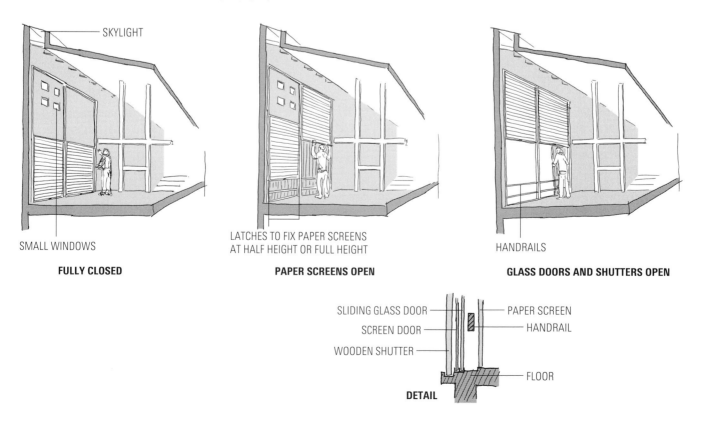

Saginomiya House, *page 22*: The roof of the living area on the second floor is supported by horizontal wooden beams. The designers have ingeniously utilized the gap formed by the beams as a source of natural light by inserting glass. The result is a band of natural light that seems to lift the ceiling from the rest of the house. Coupled with a perfectly sized garden deck, this band of windows dramatically illuminates the interior.

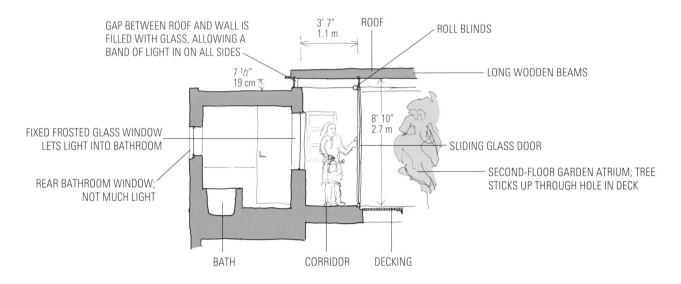

GAP BETWEEN ROOF AND WALL IS FILLED WITH GLASS, ALLOWING A BAND OF LIGHT IN ON ALL SIDES

3' 7"
1.1 m

ROOF

ROLL BLINDS

7 ½"
19 cm

LONG WOODEN BEAMS

FIXED FROSTED GLASS WINDOW LETS LIGHT INTO BATHROOM

8' 10"
2.7 m

SLIDING GLASS DOOR

REAR BATHROOM WINDOW; NOT MUCH LIGHT

SECOND-FLOOR GARDEN ATRIUM; TREE STICKS UP THROUGH HOLE IN DECK

BATH   CORRIDOR   DECKING

Ambi-Flux House, *page 62*: Although the entire Ambi-Flux House is illuminated by a wall and ceiling of glass, there was a need for artificial illumination as well. By integrating indirect fluorescent lighting with wall-mounted cabinets, the designers made the cabinets appear to float, while a gentle glow spills out from behind. As a result the walls seem to be less substantial, and the space itself seems larger.

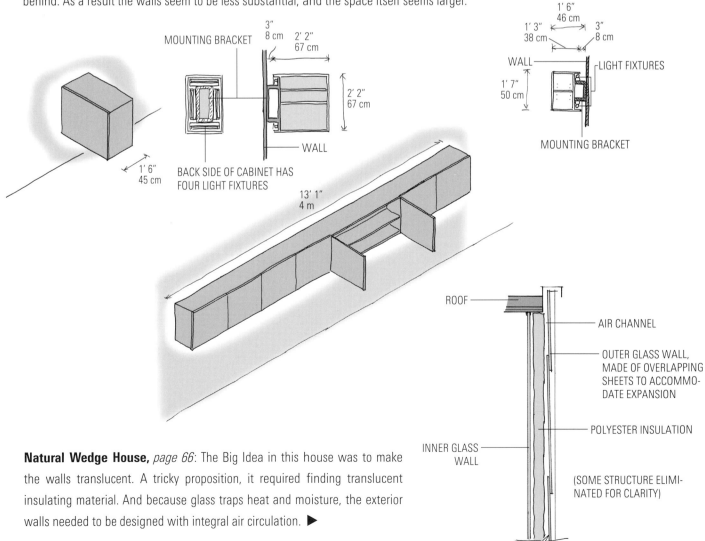

MOUNTING BRACKET

3"
8 cm

2' 2"
67 cm

2' 2"
67 cm

WALL

1' 6"
45 cm

BACK SIDE OF CABINET HAS FOUR LIGHT FIXTURES

13' 1"
4 m

1' 6"
46 cm

1' 3"
38 cm

3"
8 cm

WALL

LIGHT FIXTURES

1' 7"
50 cm

MOUNTING BRACKET

ROOF

AIR CHANNEL

OUTER GLASS WALL, MADE OF OVERLAPPING SHEETS TO ACCOMMO-DATE EXPANSION

POLYESTER INSULATION

INNER GLASS WALL

(SOME STRUCTURE ELIMI-NATED FOR CLARITY)

Natural Wedge House, *page 66*: The Big Idea in this house was to make the walls translucent. A tricky proposition, it required finding translucent insulating material. And because glass traps heat and moisture, the exterior walls needed to be designed with integral air circulation. ▶

NOOKS

Private corners for concentration

What exactly is a nook? A private space, scaled for one or maybe two people, not exactly as essential as a kitchen or bath but an important living space nevertheless. Many needs may be satisfied in a small house by including a nook of some sort. Space for work comes immediately to mind, as does space for reading or study. Perhaps the need for a guest room can be satisfied by a simple nook. Like everything else, no doubt, a good nook can only be made by considering what it attaches to, what greater hierarchy it forms a part of, and by ensuring that it adds to the overall sense of space rather than detracts from it.

White Box House, *page 58*: This desk/work area is a small tour de force. Feeling both open and protected, it is ideally scaled for one; either parent can work there while also keeping an eye on the child. Large openings and gaps allow light to filter through from the large skylight behind. The nook is part of a large unified set of built-ins that includes a counter for the TV and stereo, a cabinet for the washer, the W.C., and storage. The entire wall of built-ins is angled in plan and the ceiling slopes as well, generating a false perspective and making the space feel wider than it is.

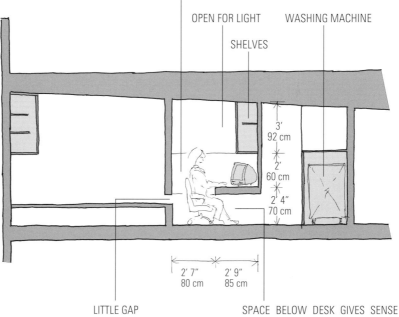

REAR PANEL GIVE A NICE SENSE OF ENCLOSURE
AND HELPS CONCENTRATION

OPEN FOR LIGHT   WASHING MACHINE

SHELVES

3'
92 cm

2'
60 cm

2' 4"
70 cm

2' 7"   2' 9"
80 cm   85 cm

LITTLE GAP

SPACE BELOW DESK GIVES SENSE
OF OPENNESS AND LETS LIGHT IN

House in Kamakura, *page 78*: After placing the bedroom under a broad sloping roof, the designer of this home turned his attention to the low-ceilinged space below. It could have been turned into a storage room as it was, but by lowering the floor a couple of feet to make a half-basement, it became an ideal basement-nook for the husband's music. Ladder rungs built into the wall make it easy and fun to climb up and down from the bedroom.

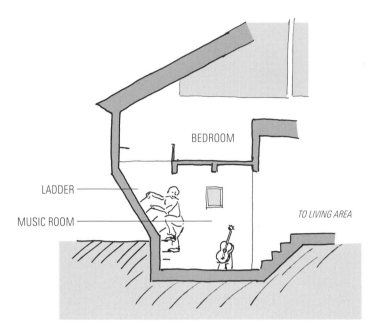

House in Kyodo, *page 74*: The architect-owner of this house wanted a comfortable but compact room for himself. With one wall lined by closets, another opening onto the study, and a third fitted with glass and movable panels to control the flow of natural light from the garden, a small section of wall was left over for air conditioning, shelves, and miscellaneous storage. By designing simple shelves with integral lighting, and matching it well with small solid and louvered sliding window panels, the result is a deluxe but spare bed nook.

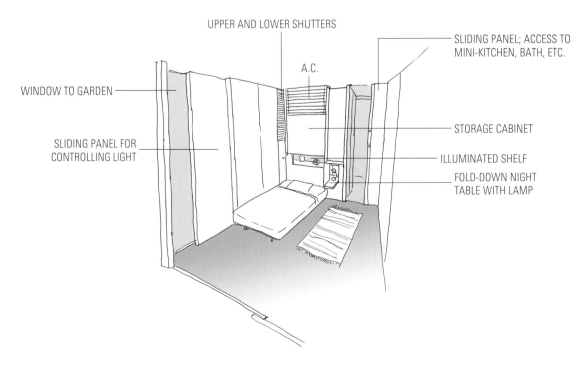

BATHROOMS
Arranging it all

Bathrooms are a necessity that seem to have some sort of inherent minimum size limit, implying that a certain amount of floor space in a new home will be occupied from the start for bathing and hygiene needs. While we have seen quite usable bath/W.C. units that take up no more than 6-by-6 feet (36 sq. ft./3.3 sq. m.), it may be safe to assume that an 8-by-8-foot (64-ft./6-m.) space will allow these needs to be taken care of comfortably if not luxuriously. All other factors must be configured to best advantage for this to work: natural light, of course, and interesting materials, especially transparent and translucent ones; flexible dividers such as curtains; necessary storage; and the overall connection of the bath area to the rest of the house. In this section a number of bath plans are compared, if only to illustrate the variety that is possible even in diminutive baths. These are Japanese bathrooms, and differ from Western ones primarily in the accommodation that is made for washing outside the tub; the Japanese bathroom is something like an oversized shower stall, large enough to place a nice tub inside. Nevertheless, many of these layout ideas will be immediately applicable to homes in other areas.

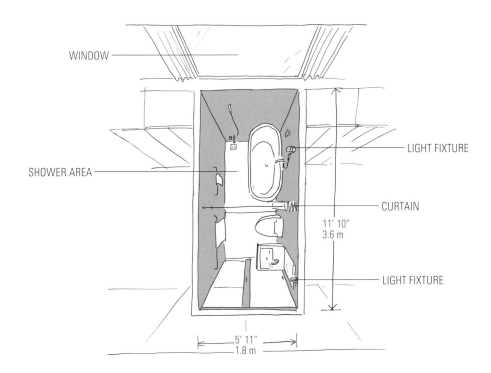

WINDOW

LIGHT FIXTURE

SHOWER AREA

CURTAIN

11' 10"
3.6 m

LIGHT FIXTURE

5' 11"
1.8 m

Engawa House, *page 86*: This unique bathroom has no ceiling and receives natural light mainly from the large windows high on the wall that serve the rest of the house. It is also a good example of combining all functions in one room—a 6-by-12-foot (1.8-by-3.6-m.) space—without using any permanent walls or partitions. A single curtain divides the bathing area from the washbasin and W.C. Some people may feel too exposed in a bathroom like this, but in fact the surrounding walls provide quite enough privacy.

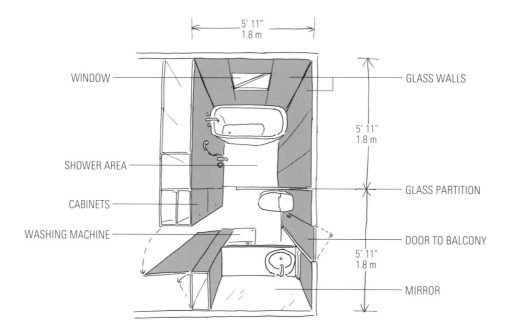

Natural Wedge House, *page 66*: The bathroom here divides a 6-by-12-foot (1.8-by-3.6-m.) rectangle into a bathing section and a washbasin/W.C. by means of a transparent glass partition. Since the walls of the house itself are glass, there is quite a lot of natural illumination, and so the partition serves mainly to give a sense of openness. The space actually is laid out in a kind of "T" with a short passageway to the small balcony outside by the space between the W.C. and the washbasin. The cabinets for towels and other supplies are small but serviceable, and a washing machine is squeezed in under the washstand.

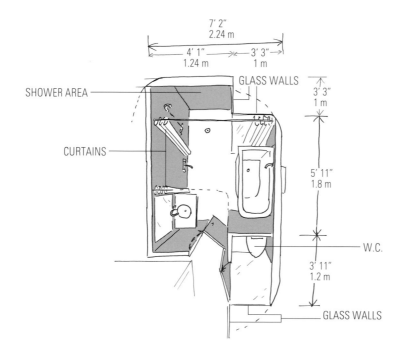

Penguin House, *page 42*: This bathroom is irregularly shaped, about 7 by 10 feet (2.2 by 3 m.), and has large full-height windows at two corners. The owners preferred the W.C. in a separate cubicle, in this case illuminated by its own glass wall. The remainder of the space is split among three functions: the washbasin, the bathtub, and a shower area. A pair of curtains provides privacy and some degree of splash protection. Extra height is gained under the walls that curve inward as they ascend.

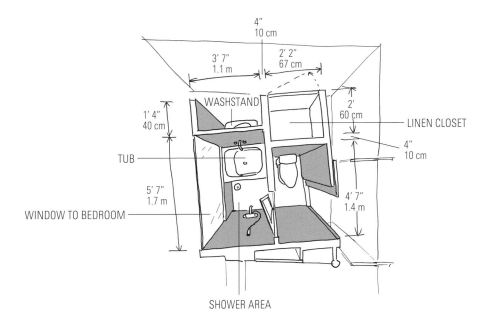

4"
10 cm

3' 7"
1.1 m

2' 2"
67 cm

WASHSTAND

2'
60 cm

LINEN CLOSET

1' 4"
40 cm

4"
10 cm

TUB

5' 7"
1.7 m

4' 7"
1.4 m

WINDOW TO BEDROOM

SHOWER AREA

House in Kyodo, *page 74*: A 5 ³/₄-by-6 ¹/₄-foot (1.8-by-2-m.) space, this bathroom is very compartmentalized and functions as a divider between two bedrooms. The bath is reached via the W.C. and has a large frosted glass window that adjoins one bedroom, through which natural light is gained. Unusually, the washstand is placed on the other side of the wall, as is the linen closet, with access from a short corridor.

ARCHITECTS' DIRECTORY AND PHOTO CREDITS

SUMIRE-AOI HOUSE
PAGES **10–11**

Architect: Makoto Koizumi
Koizumi Studio
2–2–5–104 Fujimidai, Kunitachi-shi
Tokyo 186–0003, Japan
Tel: 042–574–1458
Fax: 042–575–3646
koizumistudio@vega.ocn.ne.jp
www.koizumi-studio.jp
Photographer: Souichi Murazumi

4 X 4 HOUSE
PAGES **14–15, 19**

Architect: Tadao Ando
Photographer: Mitsuo Matsuoka

SAGINOMIYA HOUSE
PAGES **22–23**

Architects: Chiharu Sugi & Manami Takahashi
Plannet Works
Hillside Terrace A–3
29–18 Sarugaku-cho, Shibuya-ku
Tokyo 150–0033, Japan
Tel: 03–5459–1360
Fax: 03–5459–1242
plannet@vinet.or.jp
www.plannetworks.com
Photographer: Kozo Takayama

NAKAGAWA HOUSE
PAGES **26–27**

Architect: Tsuneo Shimojima
Pittori Piccoli, Inc.
2–1–11 Minami-yukigaya, Ota-ku
Tokyo 145–0066, Japan
Tel: 03–3720–5155
Fax: 03–3720–8225
shimojima@pittori.co.jp
www.pittori.co.jp
Photographs by author

HOUSE IN MOTO-AZABU
PAGES **30–31**

Architect: Mutsue Hayakusa
Cell Space Architects
3–12–3 Kugahara, Ota-Ku
Tokyo 146–0085, Japan
Tel: 03–5748–1011
Fax: 03–5748–1012
mutsu@kt.rim.or.jp
www.cell-space.com
Photographer: Satoshi Asakawa

HOUSE IN NAKA-IKEGAMI
PAGES **34–35**
HOUSE IN KAMAKURA
PAGES **78–79**

Architect: Tomoyuki Utsumi
Milligram Studio
4–2–17 Kugahara, Ota-ku
Tokyo 146–0085, Japan
Tel: 03–5700–8155
Fax: 03–5700–8156
info@milligram.ne.jp
www.milligram.ne.jp
Photographers: Takeshi Taira (p. 34 top, bottom right; p. 35 top left; pp. 78–79 all); Toru Egashira, Kodansha Shashin-bu (p. 34 bottom left, p. 35 bottom left, top right [2]); author (p. 35 bottom right [2]).

HOUSE IN UMEGAOKA
PAGES **38–39**

Architect: Mitsuhiko Sato
Mitsuhiko Sato Architect and Associates
Eiko Takanawa Bldg., 4F
2–15–15 Takanawa, Minato-ku
Tokyo 108–0074, Japan
Tel: 03–5795–4052
Fax: 03–5795–4053
msaa@msaa.jp
www.msaa.jp
Photographers: Hiroyuki Hirai (p. 38 all, p. 39 top, bottom left, middle right); author (p. 39 bottom right [2])

PENGUIN HOUSE
PAGES **42–43**

Design: Yasuhiro Yamashita / Atelier Tekuto + Masahiro Ikeda /
    Mias
Atelier Tekuto
6–15–16–301 Hon-komagome, Bunkyo-ku
Tokyo 113–0021, Japan
Tel: 03–5940–2770
Fax: 03–5940–2780
a-tekuto@mtf.biglobe.ne.jp
www5a.biglobe.ne.jp/~tekuto
Photographers: Takeshi Taira (p. 42 all; p. 43 bottom left, bottom right); Manabu Nobuto (p. 43 top)

GLASS SHUTTER HOUSE
PAGES **46–47**

Design: Shigeru Ban Architects
5–2–4 Matsubara, Setagaya-ku
Tokyo 156–0043, Japan
Tel: 03–3324–6760
Fax: 03–3324–6789
tokyo@ShigeruBanArchitects.com
Photographers: Hiroyuki Hirai (p. 46 left, top right, p. 47 top); other photos by author

T-SET HOUSE
PAGES **50–51**

Architect: Chiba Manabu Architects
Mt Harajuku Bldg., B1F
3–54–4 Sendagaya, Shibuya-ku
Tokyo 151–0051, Japan

Tel: 03–3796–0777
Fax: 03–3796–0788
manabuch@zg7.so-net.ne.jp
www.chibamanabu.com
Photographers: Nacasa & Partners (p. 50 all, p. 51 top, bottom left);
author (p. 51 bottom right)

SORA NO KATACHI HOUSE

Architect: Kazuhiko Kishimoto + Atelier Cinqu
4–15–40–403 Naka-kaigan, Chigasaki-shi
Kanagawa 253–0055, Japan
Tel: 0467–57–2232
Fax: 0467–57–2129
a-cinqu@mxc.mesh.ne.jp
Photographers: Ryo Hata (p. 54 left, top right, p. 55 top left, bottom); Kazuhiko Kishimoto (p. 55 top right, middle right); other photos by author

WHITE BOX HOUSE

Architect: Shigekazu Takayasu + Naoki Soeda / Architecture Lab
1–8–1–301 Kotobuki, Taito-ku
Tokyo 111–0042, Japan
Tel: 03–3845–7320
Fax: 03–3845–7352
takayasu@architecture-lab.com
www.architecture-lab.com
Photographer: Souichi Murazumi

AMBI-FLUX HOUSE

Design: Akira Yoneda / Architecton + Masahiro Ikeda / Mias
Architecton
1–7–16–612 Honmachi, Shibuya-ku
Tokyo 151–0071, Japan
Tel: 03–3374–0846
Fax: 03–5365–2216
a-tecton@pj8.so-net.ne.jp
Photographer: Toshihiro Sobajima

NATURAL WEDGE HOUSE

Design: Masaki Endoh / Endoh Design House + Masahiro Ikeda /
Mias
Endoh Design House
2–13–8–101 Honmachi, Shibuya-ku
Tokyo 151–0071 Japan
Tel: 03–3377–6293
Fax: 03–3377–6293
edh-endoh@mvi.biglobe.ne.jp
www.edh-web.com
Photographer: Toshihiro Sobajima

T. R. HOUSE

Architect: Yoshiaki Tezuka + Hirono Koike / K. T. Architecture
450–2–703 Nemoto, Matsudo-shi
Chiba 271–0077, Japan

Tel: 047–364–3016
Fax: 047–364–3019
Photographer: Nobuyoshi Meguro

HOUSE IN KYODO

Architect: Hoichiro Itai + Section R Architects
Villa Modeluna C–501
1–3–18 Shibuya, Shibuya-ku
Tokyo 150–0002, Japan
Tel: 03–5485–2464
Fax: 03–5485–2875
sra@tokyo.office.ne.jp
www.sra-tokyo.com
Photographer: Seiichiro Otake

HOUSE IN KAGURAZAKA

Design: Mikan
Stork Kaminoge Bldg., 3F
3–2–11 Noge, Setagaya-ku
Tokyo 158–0092, Japan
Tel: 03–5752–5490
Fax: 03–5752–5489
info@mikan.co.jp
www.mikan.co.jp
Photographers: Mikan (p. 82 all, p. 83 top left); other photos by
author

ENGAWA HOUSE

Design: Takaharu Tezuka & Yui Tezuka / Tezuka Architects +
Masahiro Ikeda / Mias
Tezuka Architects
1–29–2 Tamatsutsumi, Setagaya-ku
Tokyo 158–0087, Japan
Tel: 03–3703–7056
Fax: 03–3703–7038
tez@sepia.ocn.ne.jp
www.tezuka-arch.com
Photographer: Koui Yaginuma

KUGENUMA HOUSE

Architect: Takekazu Murayama
Murayama Architect & Associates
14–54 Mitsuzawa-shimocho,
Kanagawa-ku, Yokohama-shi
Kanagawa 221–0852, Japan
Tel: 045–316–2016
Fax: 045–314–4737
tm-arch@d6.dion.ne.jp
Photographer: Nobuaki Nakagawa

ACKNOWLEDGMENTS

I would like to thank the many people who cooperated in the making of this book, all of whom made my work easier in some way. First and foremost are the designers and owners of the featured houses, who never made me feel as though my visits were an inconvenience, and who bore my sometimes impertinent questioning with grace and good humor. I'd like to extend my deepest gratitude to my editors at Kodansha International, Barry Lancet and Nobuko Tadai, especially the latter for her tireless assistance with contacts, plans, and photographs, and for accompanying me on many house visits (and for always having a small gift for the owners). Tremendous thanks are due as well to Kazuhiko Miki, the book's designer, who is entirely responsible for the freshness of the layout. I would like to thank my assistant at the Future Design Institute, Miyako Takeshita, for lending her keen eye in visual matters and for assisting in many aspects of the production. And finally, to my student team at Kanazawa Institute of Technology for their help in the preparation of the many drawings: Yasutaka Onishi, Naoyuki Wada, Masatoshi Sakikawa, Ken'ichi Sugita, Kentaro Kawashima, Terukiyo Honma, Takeaki Zenko, Hiroshi Okada, Daisuke Ochiai, Akihito Yoshimizu, and Hirokazu Heinai.

PUBLICATION CREDITS

The publisher would like to acknowledge the following publications for permission to reprint images:

9 Tubohouse [sic] catalogue, published by commdesign Inc., Boo-Hoo-Woo.com division, pp. 10–11

Atarashii Sumai no Sekkei, published by Fuso Publishing Inc., pp. 30-31, 58-59, 66-67, 70-71, 90-91

Watanabe Atsushi no Konna Ie de Kurashitai, published by Kodansha Ltd., pp. 34 bottom left, 35 bottom left, top right (2)

Brutus, published by Magazine House Ltd., pp. 38–39

Otoko no Kakurega, published by Idea Life Co., Ltd., p. 43 top

Modern Living, published by Hachette Fujingaho Co. Ltd., pp. 62-63

Title, published by Bungeishunju Ltd., pp. 86–87

（英文版）スモールホーム　　The Very Small Home

2005 年 1 月　第 1 刷発行
2006 年 8 月　第 3 刷発行

著　者　　アズビー・ブラウン
序　文　　隈 研吾
発行者　　富田 充
発行所　　講談社インターナショナル株式会社
　　　　　〒 112-8652 東京都文京区音羽 1-17-14
　　　　　電話　03-3944-6493（編集部）
　　　　　　　　03-3944-6492（マーケティング部・業務部）
　　　　　ホームページ　www.kodansha-intl.com
印刷・製本所　　大日本印刷株式会社

落丁本・乱丁本は購入書店名を明記のうえ、講談社インターナショナル業務部宛
にお送りください。送料小社負担にてお取替えいたします。なお、この本につい
てのお問い合わせは、編集部宛にお願いいたします。本書の無断複写（コピー）
は著作権法の例外を除き、禁じられています。

定価はカバーに表示してあります。